I Think My House Is HAUNTED!

JOANNE EMMONS

Schiffer Publishing Ltd

4880 Lower Valley Road • Atglen, PA 19310

Author's Note: Many of the names in this book have been changed to protect the privacy of the individuals involved. Their stories, however, are completely true.

For the largest selection of fine reference books on this and related subjects, please visit our website at:
www.schifferbooks.com
You may also write for a free catalog.

This book may be purchased from the publisher.
Please try your bookstore first.

We are always looking for people to write books on new and related subjects. If you have an idea for a book, please contact us at
proposals@schifferbooks.com

Schiffer Books are available at special discounts for bulk purchases for sales promotions or premiums. Special editions, including personalized covers, corporate imprints, and excerpts can be created in large quantities for special needs. For more information contact the publisher.

In Europe, Schiffer books are distributed by
Bushwood Books
6 Marksbury Ave.
Kew Gardens
Surrey TW9 4JF England
Phone: 44 (0) 20 8392 8585;
Fax: 44 (0) 20 8392 9876
E-mail: info@bushwoodbooks.co.uk
Website: www.bushwoodbooks.co.uk

To my husband, Doug, for standing by my side through this crazy journey; to my stepson, Cody, for his healthy open-minded skepticism; and to my son, Dayton, whose giftedness constantly reminds me what an amazing world we live in.

Dedication

Thanks to my parents, Madeline, Al, and Bernadette, and my brother, Vince, for a lifetime of support.

Lastly to Margaret, whoever you are. You opened my eyes to all that can't be seen. May you finally rest in peace.

From the start, this journey was not one I could have made without the help of some amazing and supportive people. I would like to thank Mark Johnson for giving me my start in ghost hunting and teaching me so much.

I am also grateful to some of the most wonderful people who have shared their homes and their ghosts with me: Maria, Jeff, Kevin, and Greg in Woodbury;

Acknowledgments

Ellen and Nobby in Cedar Run; Marsha, Raymond, and McKenzie in Groveville; and Vinnie and Liz in Hillsborough.

Thanks to Debbie McGee, whose photography captures the true spirit of her subjects; Eric Rosenberg, for his meticulous editing; and Ananda, reader, advisor, and friend. Finally, I will be forever grateful to Pat Kibby and Mike Pabian, the cofounders of my own team, Paranormal Consulting & Investigations of New Jersey — you guys are the very best!

The halls of the Burlington County Prison Museum in historic Mount Holly, New Jersey, echo with the stories of those who were incarcerated there.Photo use courtesy of Board of Chosen Freeholders of Burlington County.

Contents

PREFACE

This book is designed to help you through the process of understanding and potentially living with a haunting. Whether you're at the beginning of your journey and you're questioning if you might have an unseen and uninvited house guest, or if you're convinced that your house is haunted and you want to learn more, this book will shed some light on your path. Where that road leads is up to you.

As well as discussing various aspects of ghosts and hauntings — what they are, why they're here, and what to do if you find yourself living with one — we'll also be taking an in-depth look at four families who found themselves living with very active spirits.

We'll learn about a late-1800s home that has much of its original architecture and possibly one or two of its original occupants. We will also visit a newer home shared by multiple spirits, including a little girl who has become quite attached to the woman of the house and calls her "Mommy," as well as another home built in the 1800s that was once used as an office for the nearby mill and is currently divided into several apartments. When construction began in one of the upstairs units, the spirits took out their frustrations on the unlucky tenants below. Finally, we'll meet a sensitive who has struggled to keep visiting spirits at bay.

Everyone's experience with the paranormal is different, yet there are many common threads throughout these stories that will help you to better understand your particular situation. It's human nature to fear the unknown. Many people living with a haunting experience a significant relief in their anxiety simply by gaining an understanding of ghosts in general and of their ghost in particular. For others, it's helpful just knowing that they are not alone — that what they are experiencing is not that all that uncommon. Living with the paranormal raises more questions than it answers and truly opens our minds to how much more there is in this world than we currently understand.

Introduction

A Life Touched
by Ghosts

"The mind, once expanded to the dimensions of larger ideas, never returns to its original size."

— *Oliver Wendell Holmes*

I have been fascinated by ghosts and haunted houses since I was little, but that's certainly nothing unusual. I am a full-time working mom, an engineer by education and trade. I drive a minivan and love to watch ghost shows during a quiet night at home. Still, that's nothing unusual. I've also got a beautiful home that happens to be quietly haunted, but I think that's part of why I love it. Maybe I'm a little odd. Oh, and my favorite way to spend a Saturday night is in a dark and dusty haunted attic trying to scare up a little action. Okay, so maybe that does get me part way to "unusual."

As the founder of Paranormal Consulting & Investigations of New Jersey, I am lucky that there are other equally unique people out there. Without them I would never have had the opportunity for so much field experience with ghosts and the families that live with them. Those of us who pursue the paranormal are on a quest for a better understanding of what's beyond our everyday experiences, but we each have our own story as to why we're on that journey.

In 1916, Elliot O'Donnell wrote *Twenty Years Experience as a Ghost Hunter*, which he began by explaining, "In starting a book of this sort, I believe it is usual to say something about one's self." I agree, so, in keeping with this historic tradition, I offer you my own story.

A Spirited Childhood

I was six when my family moved into a newly built house on the outer edge of a growing suburban development in Roslyn, Pennsylvania. Across the street from us, the next phase of homes had not yet been built; thus, the property was still wild and wooded. A few blocks down

was a quiet playground that my younger brother and I were eventually permitted to walk to on our own — a treasured privilege at a young age.

The simplest route there led down our street and around the corner, requiring us to pass by the neighborhood haunted house. The place had likely been the former farmhouse for the property our development overtook; in its day, it surely had been a warm and inviting sanctuary for generations of some hard-working family. Boarded up and left for dead, it was the quintessential abandoned and most certainly haunted house.

At first we would pass the place only from across the street, assuming we didn't detour our route altogether simply to avoid it. When traveling with older (or braver) friends, we would tempt fate by walking as close to the property as we could, keeping a careful eye for any movement through the windows and ready to break into a run should we hear the slightest moan from any of the ghostly inhabitants. One of the older kids always had a tale to share of children being abducted and tortured in the basement — just in case we weren't already frightened enough.

Of course there was always the dare that one of us should go inside. At first I would just pretend it was a good idea, hoping no one was really that crazy. Eventually I think I might have even been just the least bit tempted. One afternoon there were five or six of us and with strength (or stupidity) in numbers we made a pact to walk up the path, cross the porch, and try the door. If it was unlocked (and I was praying it wouldn't be), we would go in.

We had barely made it halfway up the walk before fear overtook us and the walk turned quickly into a run in the opposite direction. Each of us accused the other of being the first to turn tail, although I highly doubt I was the only one who was

A tranquil home now occupies the footprint of the old mill across from the haunted house I grew up in. *Courtesy of Pat Kibby.*

relieved when we did. In any case we never tempted fate again. Suddenly it wasn't even a topic of discussion on those sunny afternoon walks to the park.

In those days my parents carefully sheltered my brother and me from all that was scary in the world. I had never watched a horror movie or been privy to listening to adults tell spooky stories. All I knew of ghosts was that one crumbling shell of a house, where, if the stories were true, children were tortured by day and the ghosts that tormented them lurked by night.

There were exceptions. *The Addams Family* and *The Munsters* were on our list of allowed TV programs, as was *The Ghost and Mrs. Muir* — so ghosts and creepy old houses were permitted as long as they were comically entertaining. Mine was in many respects a protected and idyllic suburban childhood, for a while at least.

My parents decided to divorce when I was ten, and our beautiful Roslyn home

and the abandoned old farmhouse were both left behind. Our new life began in the historic and warmly artistic town of New Hope, Pennsylvania, a small borough nestled on the banks of the Delaware River. The house we moved into was built in 1869 and had been lovingly kept and enhanced over the years, as had the neighboring homes on our quiet little dead-end street.

The home itself was full of character, with wide planked wooden floors and many of the original doors and details. It had been built into the side of a sloping hill and overlooked the stone ruins of an old flax mill. Woods had overtaken the former mill grounds, giving us a private and picturesque view, although I often wondered if the toppling stone ruins were themselves haunted.

The failing old farmhouse and its ghostly, if imaginary, occupants were left behind and a peaceful new life began in this warm and wonderful town — except with

11

one minor caveat. The house we moved into was haunted… *Very* haunted.

In retrospect, our ghost made its presence known before we even moved in, as we were preparing the empty house for a fresh coat of paint. My mother was doing everything possible to make the move a positive experience for my brother and me and one of the little perks she offered was getting to choose our own room colors. I picked a soft pastel purple called "Grape Sherbet" while my brother went with a more traditional aqua blue. For the adjoining hall, we selected a soft harvest gold.

We began the painting preparations in my brother's room one sunny afternoon. Oddly, under each switch plate we removed we found the walls had previously been the exact same shade of light blue that we were about to apply. Next, we moved onto my room and again when we removed the first switch plate we found the same exact shade of pale purple I had selected.

I remember us all staring in disbelief for a moment and then quickly removing the electrical cover plates throughout my room. Each yielded the same result — the same shade of light purple I loved so much. Finally someone suggested we try taking off the hall switch plates. I'm sure my mother was really hoping it would take some of the weirdness away when they revealed nothing more than a dirty shade of white, but no…*not* in that house. In the hall, beneath the switch plates, was the same shade of harvest gold we had just purchased.

Of course that alone could probably have simply been chalked up to some odd coincidence if not for the things that happened over the following years. It certainly wasn't a typical symptom of a haunting. Maybe the house itself was sending us a welcoming message?

Or maybe we somehow were drawn to colors that the home or someone in it had liked? Somehow I don't think so. I believe whoever or whatever was there was letting us know of its presence — and its willingness to share their home with our family as we made it our own.

Most of the other incidents we experienced in the house were more typical of a haunting. Loud footsteps would be heard on the stairs at night and my mother would be certain it was my brother or I, but when she came to check on us we were sound asleep. Other times we would all be downstairs…only to hear loud, thudding footsteps echoing from the wooden floorboards above. My mother also remembers occasionally hearing what sounded like a large trunk being thrown down the stairs.

As is typical when ghosts are around, our dog would stare at nothingness at the end of our hallway, barking and growling incessantly. A little less typical was the time our other dog sat barking at the door to a large closet and we watched as it slowly opened on its own.…

The activity in our home could best be described as "poltergeist." Poltergeists are generally noisy and mischievous spirits and their hauntings are characterized by loud noises and moving objects. Another common manifestation with poltergeists involves opening all of the kitchen cabinets and drawers, and our spirit friend apparently found this to be amusing as well.

As is typical with poltergeist activity, things were always moving in our house. Every clock in the house would be suddenly set an hour later — even the one on the electric stove with the broken knob, requiring pliers to reset the time. (The first time this happened my mother had guests coming for dinner and was furious when they arrived an hour late or so she thought.) The next week the clocks would all be set backwards an hour.

One of the spirit's favorite tricks involved a bathroom key. The door was likely original to the home and, to get a little privacy, one needed to lock it from the inside with a small iron key. When we first moved in, my mother made a big deal of telling my brother and me how important it was not to lose the irreplaceable little thing, so of course it was a favorite pastime of our unseen friend to make it disappear on a fairly frequent basis. Sometimes it would reappear in the bathroom exactly where it was when it went missing; other times it would show up in some random spot elsewhere in the house. I blamed my brother, my mother blamed me, and someone apparently had a big laugh out of all of it.

Another favorite story of mine involves a thankfully one-time prank. My mother had already left for work one morning and my brother was desperately searching for his sneakers in time to make the bus for school. I joined in the search, but they were nowhere to be found. By that time the activity was so frequent that he remembers thinking, "Darned, now the ghost has my sneakers!" Most kids would have used that as an excuse to play hooky for the day, but not my brother — he put on his Sunday shoes and walked to school.

I was the first one home that afternoon, as usual, and had totally forgotten the morning's sneaker incident. When I went into my brother's room, I stopped dead in my tracks: There were his sneakers, right in front of the door, smack dab in the middle of his rug, placed neatly side-by-side with toes pointed toward the door! I have always thought that maybe our ghost was actually sorry for having caused so much trouble and was trying to apologize by returning them so quickly. Or maybe it just wanted us to be good and certain that

the little prank was its handiwork.

Of all the things that happened over the years, there is one I remember the most vividly, one I can find no possible explanation for even today. This was another favorite trick, performed maybe a dozen or so times in the years we were there. Our family room was at the end of a long hall with wooden floorboards, a straight shot from the hardwood stairs. Time after time everyone would be in there watching a show or playing a board game when we'd hear a quiet metallic clink-clink-clink from the hall. When we checked, we would always find the same thing — an old wheat penny. It had apparently been tossed down the stairs, bouncing along the long hall toward the room we were gathered in.

The little game, although unnerving at first, became so prevalent that we made a game of it ourselves, seeing how close to the family room the ghost would get the penny and rating each shot. It finally occurred to me one day that there may be a message in the pennies — maybe something significant about the dates or such. I saved one in a special place, and then saved the next one. The dates were different; one was from the late 1930s and the other was early 1940s. When the third penny appeared, I went to put it with the first two, but they were gone. The "game" ended soon after that.

I remember my brother and I carefully trying to recreate the penny-throwing incidents. One of us would stand at the top of the stairs and throw pennies at various angles and forces while the other was in the family room listening to see which method most closely matched the sounds we had so often heard. We weren't trying to debunk it — that would imply we were looking for a logical explanation. We had no doubt it was the ghost doing the throwing, and we were just simply trying to better understand what it took for our friend to achieve such a result. Apparently a simple toss wouldn't do it. It required more of a wrist-flicking action, like a stone being thrown to skip across a pond.

Of course we didn't become quite so comfortable with our little "ghosty" all at once, and I'm not sure my mother ever did. One of my mother's friends learned that poltergeist manifestations are a form of psychokinesis, also referred to as telekinesis, the movement or manipulation of objects by the mind without any physical contact. Psychokinetic poltergeist activity is often attributed to adolescent and pre-adolescent girls in times of stress. Being a pre-teen girl adjusting to her parents' divorce, I certainly fit the profile. Thus, my Mom's favored explanation was that this was all some psychic manifestation of my energy and would likely soon pass.

What my mother hadn't realized — and probably wouldn't have wanted to — was that the particular type of haunting we were experiencing didn't fit the profile of one that was purely psychokinetic. Still, when odd things happened, as they often did, she quietly believed I was the likely source. In her mind she must have been having an uncomfortable debate: Either ghosts really did exist and we had one sharing our home or her daughter was making some truly unnatural things happen through the power of her mind. She chose to believe the latter, and I'm not sure I can blame her.

We moved out of that house when I was fifteen, after my mother had remarried. The activity, of course, didn't stop just because we had moved. Adele Gamble runs Ghost Tours of New Hope and has been a student of the paranormal for many years, not to mention an occasional participant. Adele is also a bit, as she puts it, "intuitive." She had the opportunity to visit my former home years after I had

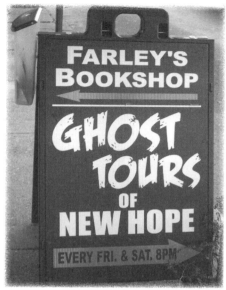

On the Ghost Tours of New Hope, you will discover both the history and the mystery of this quaint artistic town. *Courtesy of Pat Kibby*.

moved out and recalls that the downstairs was "heavy with a presence"; this was the part of the home where my brother and I both had our bedrooms and the hall was bombarded with pennies.

The rest of the story can be found in the chapter "A Ghost Named Margaret" in *Haunted Village & Valley* by Adi-Kent Thomas Jeffery and her daughter Lynda Elizabeth Jeffery. Published more than thirty years after I moved out, the stories of the subsequent owners continue where my own left off. The ghost was eventually given the name "Margaret" based on some historical research on the home's previous owners. We had no name or identity for our spirit friend when I lived there, so recently reading about Margaret all these years later was the perfect ending to my own story — as well as a fitting tribute to my dear spirit friend.

I had bought Adi-Kent Thomas Jeffery's earlier book *Ghosts in the Valley* from Farley's Bookstore in New Hope so

Farley's Bookshop has reflected the spirit of New Hope for more than forty years.

many years ago while sharing my home with Margaret, although I hadn't known her name at the time. It was also while living in that home that I knew I was going to write my own book. I started right away, scribbling down a few chapters while lying on my bed, but stopping with the realization that I hadn't yet had enough "life experience" to fill so many pages. Little did I know that Margaret had already set me on the path. In fact, I wouldn't be surprised if she even gave me the idea.

I recently drove back through my old Roslyn neighborhood where that "haunted" farmhouse had been. Sadly, it's gone now, torn down for the rest of the development that sprung up many years ago. However, ghosts usually don't go away just because their home does. There's a new home now where the farmhouse formerly stood… I often wonder if I knock on their door and ask if things go bump in the night, will they look at me as if I'm crazy or will they wonder how I knew?

Because maybe, just maybe, that old place really was haunted after all.

BELIEVING IN GHOSTS

Yes, ghosts are real. Personally I prefer to say that I know ghosts exist as opposed to that I believe in them. That implies a judgment about something personally not experienced. I used to "believe in" ghosts when I was younger. Now I simply know that they exist.

However, as certain as I may be, apparently I am in the minority. In a Rasmussen phone poll in October 2011 only thirty-one percent of Americans claimed to believe in ghosts, with another seven percent being unsure. The number of believers was up fairly significantly from previous years, with only twenty-seven percent reporting to believe in October of 2010 and twenty-three percent in October of 2009. That's a fairly substantial eight percent increase in two years. My guess is that the popularity of *Ghost Hunters* and other paranormal television shows are opening minds and creating awareness.

For the skeptics out there — those who either don't believe or are not yet quite convinced — good for you! I have no intention of trying to convince anyone that ghosts really do exist; that is simply not my purpose. However, if this book takes you even one step closer to having an open mind, I will consider that a fringe benefit.

The word skeptic comes from the Latin word *scepticus*, meaning to be thoughtful, inquiring, or reflective, and the Greek word *skeptikós*, meaning to consider or examine. In the book *Philosophy for Dummies*, the author, Dr. Thomas V. Morris, explains: "No single experience had by another person is guaranteed to change your mind, regardless of the effect it might have had on him. However, in philosophy, openness of mind is usually, as Socrates saw, a virtue. If we remain open to the new, to possibly different insights, we may be able to expand our conception of what the world is all about."

Now back to why I believe. First, there are my own personal experiences. With everything that happened to me growing up in that amazing house in New Hope, I still never actually saw a ghost or witnessed anything actually moving with my own eyes. Still, my experiences as a whole were convincing enough to leave me certain that ghosts exist. For others it might have taken a little bit more.

In the years since then, I have seen a shadow person — a dark, human-shaped figure — in my own home. I have seen a ball of light energy commonly called an orb. It was the size of a small grapefruit and I watched it travel several feet down the same hall where the shadow person was always seen. I have experienced a static feeling encompassing my body just as a psychic told me that a little girl spirit had given me a hug. I have felt a firm hand on my leg, later finding it to be relevant to the spirit thought to be in residence. I have heard a disembodied

voice, and I have attempted to walk into a room described as "feeling heavy" only to be stopped in the doorway, twice, by an unseen force in broad daylight.

The other evidence that has left me without any doubts whatsoever includes the many EVPs that my fellow investigators and I have recorded in controlled environments during investigations. EVPs, or Electronic Voice Phenomena, are voices that weren't heard at the time the recording was made but are there when the event is played back. Sometimes they are distorted or barely audible, other times they are as loud and clear as if the person was in the room with you.

On my very first investigation I was amazed, while listening to my audio recording, to hear a little girl commenting in a sing-song little voice on something a fellow investigator had just said. There were certainly no little girls in the room or even in the house at the time. When you hear EVPs presented as evidence on television shows, it's certainly intriguing, but when you record the voice of someone not present on your own recorder and that voice is clearly aware of the current situation and conversation, well it's nothing short of amazing.

My most convincing personal experience happened when I was home alone one afternoon. I was in my bathroom when I heard a loud reverberating twang maybe a foot from my left ear, a sound similar to a bass guitar string being plucked loudly. This was quickly followed by a solid thump on the side of my head, as if I had been punched in the ear but without any pain. The force went right through my skull and into my eardrum, which tingled with the impact as my head tilted from the blow.

This was probably the most unnerving thing I have experienced and it took me a few minutes just to come to grips with what had happened. Even then my eardrum still felt odd and I had to speak out loud to make sure I hadn't lost

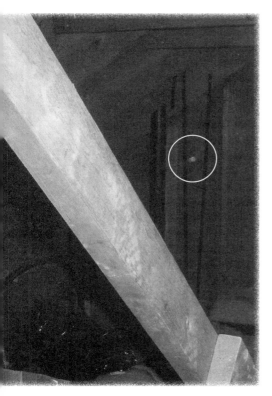

The fast movement and odd path of this orb makes it unlikely to be a dust reflection. Still, a skeptic would not be convinced.

my hearing altogether. One interpretation of the event might have been that it was an attack, but my gut feeling was that whoever it was had simply been trying to shout something in my ear.

Interestingly enough, that was only one of several unusual experiences in my house within a week, which is much more activity than we usually have in my home. We also saw doors moving on their own and a black cloud near the ceiling in our foyer shortly afterward. A few evenings later my husband watched as a man-sized shadow figure walked into the family room and disappeared into the television.

Being a ghost hunter, I do sometimes get "visitors" following me home, one of which I suspect did so — and stayed for a week! — after I had completed an investigation at the Burlington County Prison Museum in Mount Holly, New Jersey. Many prisoners spent their final days in this historic prison before being publicly hanged in the prison yard gallows. While alone in a 200-year-old cell, I saw an odd shadow pass in the darkness. I noted the apparent movement for my recording. When I later reviewed the audio file, I was surprised by what followed: An older boy's voice could be heard mournfully querying, "Mom?" It broke my heart and I've always wondered if whatever that energy was that shared my home for that week might have been this sad young man.

Of course, my experiences probably won't convince you of anything, except maybe that I might have a screw or two loose. As I mentioned before, though, convincing you that ghosts exist is not my goal. If, however, you find yourself living with things that cannot be explained, it might offer you comfort to know that many other perfectly sane people such as myself have had equally odd and unexplainable experiences. You are definitely not alone.

My husband watched from the sofa as a shadow person entered our family room from the hall and disappeared into the television.

Help! I Think My House is Haunted!

Chapter One

Ghosts? Really?

"I refuse to commit the fashionable stupidity of regarding everything I cannot explain as a fraud."

— Carl Jung

Why do ghosts fascinate us? Like scientists and philosophers throughout time, we question things in search of a deeper understanding of the world in which we live and our place in that world. Many of us have an intrinsic belief that this life we live — this current phase of our existence — is but one piece of the puzzle. Through our religious and spiritual beliefs, through meditation and mediums, and through studies of the paranormal, we seek a better understanding of all that may be. By gaining that understanding many believe we are better able to achieve whatever it is we are here to accomplish.

I have always wondered, for those lucky enough to have paranormal experiences, if they aren't little bread crumbs offered should we choose to journey down a new path. Indeed, for many, a single such experience can change the way they see the world and for some it's simply the beginning of a quest for a deeper understanding.

Most people don't remember the exact moment they began to think their house might be haunted. There may have been one incident that cinched the deal, but usually there were a lot of small events leading up to the conclusion. Often these events were accompanied by an intellectual struggle. However, once the realization is made that ghosts really do exist, an amazing journey often begins.

The earliest seed of a notion that your house might be haunted often comes when first moving in. This is especially common when work is being done to the house, whether it's a full interior renovation or simply giving a room a fresh coat of paint. Moving into a new home is a stressful process both physically and emotionally, thus in many cases the initial signs of a haunting are often missed or intentionally ignored — and why shouldn't they be? Life is in chaos, nothing is where it should be, and nothing is easy. It's difficult to recognize "abnormal" when there is no "normal," but when it is recognized, it is often tucked away in memory as something odd. Yet one odd incident does not a haunting make.

Other times a home that has been lived in for years with no signs of anything out of the ordinary suddenly starts having the unexplainable happen. Did a wandering spirit just let itself in one day and unpack his bag of tricks? It's possible, but it's more likely that your house was haunted all along and the activity has just increased enough to become noticed. Recent construction or renovations are often the culprit in such instances, but there could be other things that caused the recent rumpus.

So what are these things we call ghosts? The honest truth is that we don't really know. That's why most of us in this field call ourselves "researchers" as opposed to "experts." When it comes right down to it, we just aren't 100% sure about much of anything when it comes to the paranormal.

That said, ghosts are generally thought to be the spirits of those who have passed. However, there are other theories that are at least worth considering; residual energies, time slips, parallel universes, and extraterrestrials are some favorites. Once we do get this all figured out, the vast array of happenings that we currently lump under the topic of "paranormal" will likely involve a few of these theories. Although paranormal researchers are not all in complete agreement, there is a commonly accepted view of the type of hauntings and spirits one may encounter.

Residual Hauntings

In residual hauntings, the manifestations — whether sightings, sounds, or smells — are repeated over and over like a tape looping. Some can be echoes of a human behavior repeated again and again over the years, such as a woman in period clothing approaching the mantle at the same time each night, raising a hand and leaning forward as if snuffing out a candle, before vanishing into thin air. Some are associated with a single intense experience, such as a horrible thudding down the stairs where a man once fell to his death as his wife looked on in horror or, perhaps, in triumph. Others are simple, lingering moments: a whiff of perfume, a riff of music, or the sound of a child's ball bouncing.

However, residual hauntings are usually not attributed to the spirit of a person. They are thought to be more like a snapshot or a hologram of a once-living person reliving a daily ritual or a tragic occurrence.

A few commonalities of residual hauntings are that they are usually repeated, although we may not be aware of each repetition, and the spirit in these hauntings have absolutely no interaction with us. There is certainly nothing to fear with these types of occurrences because they can't hurt us in any way and, since they are simply repeated playbacks of some moments in time, most investigators say there is nothing that can be done to get rid of them. They may fade away over the months or years, wax and wane in frequency, or suddenly cease altogether. In any case they are one of the great mysteries of the paranormal.

Intelligent Hauntings

An intelligent haunting is one in which the ghost or spirit is as aware of us as we are of them, sometimes more so. Unlike residual hauntings, they may manifest in multiple locations and in a multitude of ways. They often try to make themselves known by interacting with our environments: messing with our electronics, knocking on walls, hiding things, slamming doors, or even waking us up in the middle of the night. We may see shadows out of the corner of our eye or even a full-bodied apparition. If a ghost turns to look straight at you, it is likely one we would refer to as "intelligent."

Not all intelligent spirits try to invoke interaction, though. Some seem to be content to stay out of the limelight, to just be in their own world, whatever that world might consist of. You may catch a glimpse of them once in a while or otherwise notice their presence, but that is likely not their intent. They just seem to share our homes in their own quiet way. Maybe they simply don't have the energy to manifest, or maybe that's how they were in life — quiet and unassuming, preferring to be left to themselves.

Although this convenient and simple differentiation between residual and intelligent hauntings has been well accepted for years, there are instances that don't quite fit so cleanly, reminding us that all we think we understand is not all there is to know. One interesting example is the ghost of the Sentry guarding the cupola at the top of Pennsylvania Hall at Gettysburg College. This young man's apparition would commonly be classified as residual; it is seen pacing back and forth on the cupola still on guard after almost 150 years. However, on rare occasions he has been spotted aiming his rifle at specific students on the ground. Maybe the difference between residual and intelligent isn't as clear-cut as we would like to believe.

Crossed-Over vs. Earthbound

When we consider spirits of the intelligent variety, one common perspective is to classify them as earthbound or crossed over. Earthbound spirits are what we typically think of with hauntings — they are generally thought to be the spirit of someone who, upon the death of their physical body, has not crossed over to the great beyond and is now wandering the earth disembodied.

Crossed over spirits are entirely different. Interactions with this type of spirit are generally referred to as "visitations." These spirits have made the journey to the other side and are sometimes able to come to visit us, usually to bring peace or comfort, but sometimes offering insight, information, or occasionally a warning.

There are a few ways to tell the difference between an earthbound spirit and a visitation from a crossed-over one, but frequency is one clue. Crossed-over spirits simply don't hang around all the time as earthbounds do. They may appear in a dream or by our bedside, or we may

Stairwells are often the scene of paranormal activity, both residual and intelligent. Is it possible that the shape of these structures amplifies their energy in some way?

catch a whiff of their cigar smoke when no one is around or even simply sense their comforting presence. They may even leave a trinket that will remind you of them for you to find or offer other signs of their

This frame is from a video that captured a moving flash of light. Later in the evening two other bright flashes were captured on these stairs where a girl's spirit is thought to dwell.

presence, but they are simply visiting and are not constantly lurking around our homes. If you hear footsteps in an unoccupied bedroom every night, if the television comes on by itself even after you replaced it and had the wiring checked, if the dog is continually watching things that aren't there, then it's doubtful you are simply experiencing a visitation from a loved one.

Another differentiation is in the spirit's intent. Crossed-over spirits have made the transition to a greater state of consciousness. If they come to visit us, it is only ever with good intentions. There is no revenge or hatred or jealously from a crossed-over spirit — just love, peace, and compassion.

In contrast, an earthbound spirit will be just the same as the day they died. If they were sweet and maternal, you will have a sweet maternal ghost. If they were mean or angry or even prejudiced in life, then that is exactly what you get from their earthbound spirit. A crossed-over spirit is there to offer you something. An earthbound spirit is generally self-focused and is not hanging around to provide any benefit to the living. However, this does not mean they won't form a friendly attachment or warn you if their beloved house is at risk of catching fire. It just means that they are not on any sort of mission to help or comfort you — their journey is their own.

Crossed-over spirits, earthbound ghosts, and even demonic entities can all enter our dreams. Earthbounds and demonic entities often cause nightmares. In these cases the dreams will be convoluted and morphing as typical dreams and nightmares are, and are difficult to distinguish from any other dream. When crossed-over spirits visit us in our slumber, the dreams tend to be much more lucent and vivid.

Poltergeists

One other type of haunting worth mentioning is that of a poltergeist. Poltergeists, or "noisy spirits," have a greater ability to physically affect the world around them than a typical spirit might. The hallmarks of a poltergeist haunting are generally loud noises and objects being moved. In more extreme cases cabinet doors may be found open, objects can fly across a room, and heavy furniture may be found moved.

Parapsychologists often make a distinction by classifying situations with such activity into those due to psychokinesis and those associated with an actual spirit. As mentioned before, psychokinesis is a phenomenon where physical objects are moved by the power of the mind, with a specific person, referred to as an "agent," at the focus of the activity. These agents are often adolescent or preadolescent girls, but this is far from a hard criteria. Another lesser common attribute of agents is that they sometimes have disturbances of the central nervous system, such as seizures or epilepsy. Agents are also often found to be under some sort of stress.

Psychokinetic poltergeist activity is distinguishable from poltergeist-like spirit activity in several ways. According to William Roll, the activity is usually shorter in duration, often lasting a week or two or possibly as long as a few months. Spirit hauntings last for much longer periods of time. With pyschokinetic poltergeist hauntings, the activity itself is usually more frequent and often more forceful than with a spirit haunting. It is also centered on a specific person and ceases when that person is not around. A spirit haunting will usually continue regardless of the specific individuals present. Often, the psychokinetic-based activity will start small and then escalate quickly.

According to Psychiatrist Ian Stevenson, psychokinetic poltergeist activity can be distinguished from spirit activity simply by the type of object movement; in poltergeist cases the movement of objects is without purpose and often violent while cases involving spirits of the dead involve intelligent communication, purposeful movement of objects, and little violence.

Characteristics of a Psychokinetic Poltergeist Haunting

- Shorter in duration, typically weeks to months
- Frequent manifestations
- Activity usually happens with a specific person present
- Starts with small things but escalates quickly
- Violent and seemingly random object movement, such as objects flying off shelves

Characteristics of a Spirit Poltergeist Haunting:

- Longer in duration, often lasting for years
- Manifestations are fairly infrequent
- No specific person need be present for activity to occur
- Manifestations may increase and decrease over time
- Purposeful object movement such as personal items being hidden

Parapsychologists typically restrict the term "poltergeist" to those cases involving psychokenisis and call similar manifestations due to ghosts simply "a haunting." However, mainstream use of the term "poltergeist" often refers to any haunting that is noisy, particularly active, and involves the movement of objects. Therefore, in understanding a case with poltergeist-like symptoms, it is important to distinguish if the activity is potentially pyschokinetic or if there is indeed a spirit involved. Cases involving psychokinetic poltergeist activity merit special attention.

Crisis Visitations

"Crisis Visitations" is the name most commonly used for visitations of one sort or another just shortly before or after the time of a loved one's death. They can take the form of visions of the person or even entire conversations with them, usually with no clue at the time that the person has just passed on. Sometimes they come as phone calls with only static, or with no one at all on the other end of the line. Other times they involve cryptic messages or perfectly "normal" conversations. It is only afterwards when we learn that our loved one has passed that we realize that our final encounter was not a typical one.

I had a dear friend, Tom, whom I had worked with in a restaurant while living in Mississippi. We had kept in close touch when I moved to Ohio, speaking on the phone, sometimes every few weeks, sometimes every month or so, but it was never long between calls.

Early one Sunday, around 2 a.m., I found myself unable to sleep. I remember getting up to go to the bathroom, though not really having to go. When I walked in, instead of taking care of business I found myself sitting cross-legged on the floor opening the cabinet doors under the sink. I had moved to Ohio a good six months prior, but there was a small box of bathroom odds and ends that had been shoved in the back of the cabinet and never unpacked.

I pulled the box out and began digging through it, stopping when I came across a bottle of perfume. Spraying a little on, I tucked the bottle back in the box and returned to bed. The perfume had been an inadvertent gift from Tom as he happened to draw my name in a company Christmas Pollyanna. I had worn it almost daily to my waitressing job and the familiar smell instantly brought back a flood of memories of Tom and the times we spent together.

It wasn't until two weeks later when I hadn't heard from Tom for a while that I called the restaurant he worked at — only to be told he had passed in a car accident leaving work two weeks before. He had apparently stayed after-hours hanging out with his friends; sadly the car he was in had hit a semi head-on while on their way home at 2 o'clock in the morning.

It was no coincidence that I was drawn to dig in an odd box under the sink that night just as Tom had met his tragic end here on Earth. He found an amazing way to leave me with such special memories of our times together as a final goodbye and I have always been so thankful for that.

Negative, Non-Human, or Demonic Hauntings

In many of my conversations about ghosts and hauntings, the subject of evil spirits eventually comes up. As many questions as I get asked about the paranormal, though, I am rarely asked if negative or demonic entities exist. More typically I hear something more cautiously along the lines of "You know evil spirits exist, right?" Yes, unfortunately they do.

Before we delve into a conversation on how to tell if your particular haunting might be negative — and luckily the great majority of them are not — let's clarify some of the terminology often used.

The term "negative haunting" is used to define one that has unwelcome and hurtful aspects, such as scratching or pinching, but which may not be demonic or non-human. The haunting may simply be due to an earthbound spirit, just one who is, to put it mildly, not very nice. The Groveville case we will be reviewing in Chapter 11 is a good example of a negative haunting. In fact, the client nicknamed the offensive spirit "Mr. Grumpy Pants."

"Non-Human" refers to any type of haunting that is not attributed to the spirit of someone once living. It's a broad category including everything from angels to demons as well as fairies, elementals, and other such creatures. Typically, though, when we talk about non-human hauntings we are referring to demonic entities.

Demonic entities are non-human beings that have absolutely no good in them. They often haunt individuals weakened by alcoholism, drug addiction, or some other emotional or psychological condition. If you suspect that you may be dealing with a demonic entity, seek professional help immediately.

Demonic hauntings differ from traditional hauntings in several ways. Initially they may behave as any other intelligent haunting with the demon likely making an effort to appear sweet and innocent. In demonic hauntings, though, the activity will often escalate quickly, becoming dramatic and often violent. Demonic entities also tend to target specific individuals and will often attempt to isolate one member of the family.

Other symptoms of a
demonic haunting are:

- *Physical attacks such as scratches, punctures, welts, or being slapped*
- *Putrid smells reminiscent of sulfuric acid, rotting eggs, or rotting flesh*
- *Growling sounds coming from anywhere or seemingly everywhere*
- *Onsets of unexplained negative emotions such as anger or hatred, often accompanied by thoughts of violence*

Demonic hauntings can be dangerous and need to be dealt with immediately by trained professionals.

OTHER THEORIES ABOUT GHOSTS AND HAUNTINGS

As much as we think we know when it comes to ghosts and hauntings, we likely have at least part of it all wrong. Lest we become too complacent with our current views of the paranormal, it is worthwhile to consider alternate theories other than the spirits of the dead.

Although my personal belief is that much of the paranormal phenomena we encounter as ghost hunters are the spirits of those who have died and not yet crossed over, I certainly don't believe these spirits account for all of the paranormal activity in this world. There is so much we don't understand. The following is only the briefest of glimpses into some fascinating theories on the subject.

Time Slips

Time slips can be thought of as anomalies in the fabric of time, permitting the past and present to briefly intertwine. Stories have been told throughout history of people happening upon a scene form the distant past, sometimes even visiting towns or staying in hotels that no longer exist, although the visitors were often unaware of this little detail at the time of their stay.

When we see a ghost are we simply witnessing a time slip and being granted a peak at some moment in the past, or possibly even in the future? When we capture voices of those not present on our recorders, might not these voices be simply slipping through some small hole in the fabric of time itself?

Parallel Universes

The theory of parallel universes postulates that our physical existence may not be the only one. If there are other universes or dimensions, could ghosts not simply be people just like us, living in one of these alternate realities? Maybe our worlds are separated by a thin veil and at times, if some yet unknown conditions are just right, the veil briefly parts. Given this theory it would be possible that you and I have at some time been ghosts in someone else's world as well.

Extraterrestrials

Consider for a moment that there may be other planets in our universe and that these planets might be populated with advanced intelligent beings. Now, imagine that this species has evolved past the need for a physical body and can exist purely as energy. Might it not be possible then that these beings, these energies, can and do visit us here on Earth for whatever reason they may have? When we see an orb, maybe it's simply the energy of some such being. If extraterrestrials are watching us, even studying us, it's a bit presumptuous to assume that these highly evolved beings would require a spaceship, or even a physical body, to do so.

Our Own Manifestations

Maybe ghosts don't come from another time or place or dimension. Maybe they are just physical manifestations from our own minds. Our brains are indeed powerful sources of energy and we are only beginning to understand how that power can be harnessed. It isn't too much of a stretch to imagine that this energy could somehow take physical form, maybe to manipulate a recording device with a voice, to create the image of someone we are subconsciously thinking of, or to simply manifest as a flash of light or an orb.

Similarly, it is possible that our own energy, especially when our emotions are extreme and running deep, can leave a footprint much like how our voices leave physical impressions on recorders. Maybe residual hauntings are simply emotional energy footprints

recorded and played back by some yet not-understood means. If so, then it's possible the energy we're creating at this moment can be reflected back to us in a more "live" playback mode, thus creating what we currently think of as intelligent spirits.

Each of these theories could fill an entire book. There certainly isn't space here to do any of them justice. Just remember this: If you're experiencing paranormal activity, don't rush to immediately interpret it as an earthbound spirit without a little consideration for other possible explanations.

Chapter Two

Ghosty, Are You There?

---

*"I often think that the night is more alive and more
richly colored than the day."*

— *Vincent Van Gogh*

Ghosts can be — and are — found just about anywhere: from ship to shore, from rural farmhouses to urban high-rises, from locations seeped in history to those with brand new housing developments. There just doesn't seem to be a lot of rules preventing them from roaming as far and wide as the living themselves. If you name a type of location, someone somewhere very likely has a ghost story about just such a place. Still, certain types of locations are more likely to be haunted than others.

No matter where you are when you run into a ghost, the *most* unnerving thing is often that you weren't expecting it. Okay, maybe that's not the most unnerving thing, but it does add to the overall effect. Wherever you go you run the risk of coming face-to-face with a wandering spirit. For the most part, if we do get any indications of their presence — a cold spot rushing past us or unexplained sounds in our hotel room at night — we often don't give it a second thought. If most mediums are to be believed, though, spirits are all around us. Somehow I don't doubt that.

Home is Where the Ghost Is

The most traditional type of haunting is a haunted house. From cottages to castles, the dead still seem to prefer to dwell at home. Usually a resident ghost can be traced back to someone who died in the home, but that isn't always so. People who have left home to spend their final days in a nursing home have still been known to return to their former abodes upon leaving their bodily restraints. Even those who have had a more untimely passing far from home sometimes still return post-mortem.

Just because a house had no previous occupants that have passed on doesn't mean it can't be haunted. As we'll see

in our Cedar Run case in Chapter 10, even a new home still occupied by the original owners can attract a ghost now and then.

Spirits can end up in your home in many ways. They may be attached to the land the home was built on or to an object brought into the home, or can even follow someone home like a curious puppy. They can be invited in as well, often through a portal opened in a séance or with an Ouija Board.

Historical and Battlefield Hauntings

Throughout history there have been deadly events so emotionally charged that they have left a permanent footprint on the location. Historic locations associated with wars or battles are often the most notoriously haunted. Given the magnitude of the physical and emotional pain condensed in both time and location, it is hard to imagine the events not having some sort of long-term effect. If you visit such a location, keep your eyes peeled and your ears open. You might hear a cry of defeat or the echo of a cannon from days long gone, or perchance witness a hapless soldier or even an entire brigade.

Gettysburg, Pennsylvania, is perhaps one of the most notoriously haunted towns associated with such a battle. In June 1863, Gettysburg was just a small market town of 2,400. The Civil War was well underway when General Robert E. Lee's Confederate Army and General George G. Meade's Union Army met there by chance on July 1st, after a Confederate brigade, sent in search of shoes, spotted Union soldiers. In the following days, more men fought and died in that fateful town than in any other battle in American history. By

As re-enactors fire their muskets during a scripted battle, are the ghosts of Confederate soldiers taking up arms alongside them? *Photo courtesy of Paul Witt*.

The Cashtown Inn is considered to be one of the most haunted places in Gettysburg. The inn has been featured on the Travel Channel and SciFi Channel's *Ghost Hunters*.

some accounts, almost 8,000 souls took their final breath on Gettysburg's soil. If you visit this historic town, please respect both their preservation attempts and the spirits of those who remain.

Just days before the historic battle, Confederate Lt. General A. P. Hill and his troops occupied the Cashtown Inn and set up their headquarters, marking the second occupation of the town by rebel troops since the war began. During the battle, the inn served as a makeshift hospital for injured soldiers, with surgeries and amputations performed in the basement. Some say every room in the Cashtown Inn is haunted. If that's true, who would be surprised given such a history?

The Cashtown Inn is but one Gettysburg location with a story to tell and a spirited atmosphere. Throughout the world battlefields and locations with historical significance and an undertone of death seem to echo the events back through time as a reminder of what is not to be forgotten.

The Logan Inn's sign boasts "Fine Food * Spirits * Lodging" … right on all accounts. *Photo courtesy of Pat Kibby.*

Inns and Hotels

Inns and hotels are probably the most common location for experiencing paranormal activity away from the home. After all, you're there all night. Not only are paranormal encounters more frequent after dark, but the quiet backdrop of the overnight hours means you're more likely to notice anything unusual. Many people have checked into some of these spots as skeptics and checked out as complete believers — that is if they bother to check out at all on their way out the door in the middle of the night!

John Wells, the founder of New Hope, Pennsylvania, originally built the Logan Inn as a tavern in 1722. He later converted it to an inn as it was conveniently located by the ferry shuttling passengers across the Delaware River on the trek between Philadelphia and New York. The historic inn has seen more than its fair share of American history, being a mere ten miles upriver from where George Washington and his brave men crossed the Delaware to defeat the Hessian forces on that fateful Christmas Eve of 1776. Two years later General Washington and his troops passed through New Hope on their way to their winter encampment in Valley Forge.

The inn today has maintained its Colonial styling and the ambiance is warm, welcoming, and unassuming. With the Revolutionary War being such a large part of the area's history, the ghostly soldier purportedly taking refuge in the bar and basement of the inn should come as no surprise. The Logan Inn boasts sixteen spacious guest rooms, each furnished with colonial period pieces and antiques, but Room 6 is the place to stay if you're looking for a different kind of a night life in New Hope.

Having run the Ghost Tours of New Hope for twenty-five years, Adele Gamble knows the Logan Inn well and has her own story to share about her stay in Room 6. She was relaxing in a comfortable chair one evening when she felt the temperature of the room drop noticeably, followed by the apparition of a man, woman, and child in varying degrees of transparency. Adele asked them why they were there; she told her that they were "travelers" and were just passing through.

Room 6 had long ago belonged to Emily, the mother of one of the inn's former owners, who died peacefully on the property of old age. The room is still adorned with her original furniture and she often "visits" those who come to stay. The next time you're in New Hope, be sure to book a room at the Logan Inn, but if you choose Room 6, be prepared to share. Apparently a few of the previous occupants aren't quite ready to checkout.

Graveyard Hauntings

For thousands of years graveyards have been feared and avoided, as spirits were thought to return to the place of their death or burial. As early as the fourth century BCE, Plato warned against hanging out in such places. In his dialogue "Phaedo," he explains "…it haunts, as men say, monuments and tombs; by these have been seen shadowy forms of souls, apparitions such as souls of this kind provide when they are separated from the body."

According to renowned medium Mary Ann Winkowski, consultant to CBS's *Ghost Whisperer*, graveyards are simply not the ghostly romping grounds that they're often made out to be.

Contrary to popular belief, cemeteries are not the most haunted spots on earth. Other than ghosts who attend their graveside services, it is uncommon to find an earthbound spirit hanging around a graveyard. A ghost – most often an older person – may stop by the cemetery on occasion to see if his or her gravesite is being properly tended to by the family.

Mary Ann is, however, referring to earthbound ghosts. Crossed-over spirits may know when you stop by their grave for a visit and might well join you. Of course they can — and do — join you other times just as easily. Be it a wedding or a birthday, or just a rainy Sunday at home, they are often with us, so a visit to their bodily final resting place is no different.

Still, many ghost hunters love a good graveyard investigation when they just want to have a little fun, and the evidence often makes it worth their while. On one particular visit to my father-in-law's grave I placed a recorder on his headstone, hoping for a message of some kind. My husband, my son and I were a few feet away and with the occasional gusts of wind we could hardly be heard on the recording. No one else was within at least a hundred yards. Yet when I played back the recording there was a clear but quiet voice, that of a younger man and one that most definitely was not my father-in-law. The odd EVP began with the sound of an old-fashioned phone ringing and then, as if answering, a disembodied voice announced "Hey there mother f*&#@!". No, most certainly not my father-in-law.

I have no worries about the kind of neighbors my father-in-law is sharing his final resting place with, though. Earthbound spirits don't vocalize phone ringing sounds, so whatever I happened to capture was likely just a little slice of time and place that somehow made its way through to the here-and-now.

Theaters

Theaters are notorious for being haunted, with many people having experiences that they cannot explain in these buildings. It's really not that surprising when you think about it — acting itself is a hugely emotional experience. When on-stage, actors put everything they have into a performance and, when you think about it, that's a lot of emotional energy expelled day after day, year after year. If a soul loved the theater, it would be a perfect place to return after death, and for the living it is often a perfect place to run into the dead.

One of my favorite theaters, the Cincinnati Music Hall, was completed in 1878 and more than qualifies for having a long history of emotional performances, quite enough to fuel any ghostly appetite. However, that is not all of it. This beautiful architectural building was built on top of a pauper's cemetery where the indigent and homeless of Cincinnati were buried, often in unmarked graves. While digging an elevator shaft in the late 1980s, over two hundred pounds of human bones were discovered. It's certainly not surprising, given the circumstances, that the music hall is purportedly quite haunted. In fact the stories started before construction was even completed. If you are ever in Cincinnati, get a ticket and enjoy a show. The architecture itself is worth the price of admission. Just remember to keep an eye out for extras.

SEEKING SPIRITS

Some people have no intention of waiting to happen upon a ghost, preferring instead to seek them out. With the popularity of ghost hunting shows, an increasing number of people want to have their own paranormal experience. As supply often follows demand, many haunted locations have started teaming up with paranormal investigators offering a chance to participate in your own live ghost hunt — for a fee, of course.

These experiences can range from educational ghost hunting introductions to noisy, overcrowded events where if you did have any ghostly activity it would be quite difficult to tell, but many are well conducted, interesting, fun, and sometimes eventful. Even experienced ghost hunters enjoy them from time-to-time — and for those who do take advantage of the opportunity, it often turns a skeptic into a bona fide believer.

One Skeptic's Story...

Janine is a fairly typical skeptic. Or at least she used to be. She's a middle school teacher, a structured, patient, educated woman, and not apt to believe much of anything without a little something to back up the claim.

Janine's parents weren't believers in the paranormal. They didn't discuss ghosts at the dinner table, except, of course, to caution her *not* to go into the woods or the Jersey Devil would get her — certainly not an uncommon warning for those growing up in New Jersey. She does, however, clearly recall one story.

Her grandmother told her of a time when, long before, she had been in bed, nursing the latest addition to the family, eyes shut from exhaustion, while her five other children played in the house. One particular child kept popping in for one thing or another, so she wasn't surprised to feel the bed depress slightly as someone sat next to her. She scolded the child to leave her alone, but when she opened her eyes she was quite surprised to see not a child but a Native American woman sitting next to her in the bed.

Janine, being a very logical child, had always just assumed that the exhaustion of childbirth and mothering six children had taken its toll on her grandmother. She didn't believe the poor woman was making the story up, but it certainly didn't convince her that ghosts are real.

Janine's friend Elexis, a science teacher, has a much different perspective on ghosts, although her opinions have been bolstered by personal experiences. Elexis loves to go on ghosts hunts, and, like most in the field, approaches them from a very scientific perspective. She managed to talk Janine into joining her on a paid ghost hunt at the Philadelphia Zoo.

On the drive there, Elexis shared the story of another investigation she'd been on at Eastern State Penitentiary in Philadelphia, Pennsylvania, with renown medium Chip Coffey, and of a conversation — via a K-II meter and a flashlight — with a spirit they learned had been locked up for stealing to support his family. The spirit of this man had been very cooperative that evening in turning the flashlight on and off to converse with Elexis. Of course to Janine all this talk of flashlights going on and off by themselves was a little out there. Thus Janine began the trip to the zoo thinking her friend maybe had one too many bats in her belfry.

As well as achieving notoriety as the first zoo in America, having opened its gates in 1874, the Philadelphia Zoo has also become famous for its ghosts. The Sci-fi Network's *Ghost Hunters* had filmed an episode there, and when Janine and Elexis arrived at the site they began their evening with a viewing of the show, which showed its stars investigating the same areas they were about to explore.

Shortly afterwards, they headed out on their own and wound up alone on the second floor of the Penrose building, formerly the research lab and veterinary hospital for the zoo. They set up shop in a conference room and Elexis did an EMF sweep (a measure of Electromagnetic Field energy) to get a baseline and noted nothing unusual. She placed her K-II meter and flashlight on the conference table, introduced herself to no one in particular, and began attempting to talk to whatever spirits might be listening. Seeing her otherwise scientific and level-headed friend talking to people who weren't there, Janine mentally confirmed her earlier suspicions. She was also questioning her own sanity for having paid good money to sit in the dark listening to her friend talking to ghosts and expecting a response.

Elexis continued talking to thin air; she introduced Janine and explained that they were just here because they were curious. She also mentioned that Janine was a skeptic and asked unseen forces to turn on the flashlight. For maybe five minutes there was nothing...and then the flashlight came on.

As Janine tells it, she almost wet her pants as she grabbed for Elexis. It's always nice when your first time is with someone a little more experienced who is unlikely to freak out at a little paranormal activity, so Janine was in good company. She was just with a little more company than she had expected.

Elexis, as any good ghost hunter would, calmly asked whoever-it-was to turn the flashlight back off. Not only did it comply, but the flashlight rolled off the table with a loud thud — and just to add a secondary affirmation, the K-II meter was flashing away.

During that one memorable evening, Janine, a pretty and intelligent middle school teacher, had been taught a little something and, as always, she was a quick learner. She began the evening with an open mind, although she was fairly sure this ghost stuff was all just a flight of fantasy. She ended the night with the knowledge that there is more to the world then our senses can perceive and that maybe, just maybe, her grandmother wasn't seeing things after all.

Having been indoctrinated at the Philadelphia Zoo, Janine soon signed up for a second adventure with Elexis — a paid investigation at Eastern State Penitentiary where Elexis had been before. Janine was struck by the place, its history, and the lingering traces of those who called the place home so long ago — for many, it was their last. The investigation that night had been fairly uneventful and by midnight Janine was feeling the effects of the long day. Her stomach was bothering her, and she was antsy and ready to go. To make it worse, the anxious feeling she sometimes gets had come over her.

Elexis was making the most of their remaining time there. With her K-II meter at hand, she settled down in a cell with a bench, placed a red flashlight and a black one some distance apart, and asked whoever was there to turn on the black flashlight. Suddenly Janine's entire emotional state changed. A feeling of calmness came over her and her stomach ache vanished. Even her anxiety was gone, replaced with a feeling that everything was going to be okay. She found herself smiling, overtaken with a happy giddy feeling.

As if to confirm that some external forces were at work, the red flashlight came on — not the black one as Elexis had requested. Elexis quickly asked the spirit to turn the red flashlight back off and instead the black one came on. Someone was in a very playful mood. For a bit then, it was like a light show, with the flashlights turning on-off, on-off, on-off. Janine and Elexis both just ended up laughing. Apparently ghosts aren't all about gloom and doom.

Does the stunning architectural design of Cellblock 5 at Eastern State Penitentiary echo the energy of those who died there? *Photo courtesy of Elena Bouvier and Eastern State Penitentiary Historic Site in Philadelphia, Pennsylvania.*

Chapter Three

Is My House Haunted?

"When you have excluded the impossible, whatever remains, however improbable, must be the truth."

— *Sherlock Holmes by Sir Arthur Conan Doyle*

What does it mean when we say a house is haunted? As with much non-standardized terminology, different people tend to use the term in different ways. Many ghost investigators, for example, will often present their findings as "paranormal" as opposed to stating outright that the house is "haunted" — unless there is measurable and significant evidence of an intelligent spirit. The layperson, on the other hand, may refer to his or her house as being haunted simply because he or she may have experienced some unexplainable events. Although neither may be wrong, the term "haunted" itself leaves a lot of room for interpretation.

Generally speaking, a house isn't considered to be haunted if the activity appears to be residual, even though we often do call it a "residual haunting." Most professionals require some evidence of intelligent spirit interaction to consider using the term "haunted" in their findings.

Another criterion for a haunting is that the activity must last over a long period of time. Again, there are no set standards here. If you experience a few weeks or even a few months of seeing shadows, hearing noises, or catching glimpses of a full-bodied apparition, that does not necessarily mean your house is haunted. You may simply be experiencing a visitation or some other transitory state that we do not yet fully understand. The term "haunted" is typically reserved for a more enduring situation.

Finally, most investigators also need some level of significance or intensity of the manifestations to call a house haunted. Even if evidence is captured that indicates an intelligent interaction, and even if there were significant paranormal experiences during the investigation, some groups will still present the client with the verdict of having "paranormal activity" as opposed to stating that their house is indeed haunted. "Haunted" implies a resident ghost, and groups that take a purely scientific approach are not always willing to jump to the conclusion that a spirit is the source of the paranormal activity, even if they think that's likely. There is just so much we still don't know.

Rightly so, most paranormal investigation teams require evidence that they themselves capture and can vouch for when assessing whether a house is experiencing paranormal activity. However, the inverse doesn't hold; if the investigating team doesn't find any evidence of the paranormal, it doesn't mean that there isn't a resident spirit — only that they weren't able to find an indication of one. Spirits can *and do* make themselves scarce on occasion.

What if you believe you're living with a ghost, but have never had a formal investigation done and have no proof? Well, I leave it to you to decide. If you have done your homework and you are still convinced that you share your home with some earthbound spirit, then feel free to consider your house to be haunted.

How might you know if your house is haunted? Just as there are many ways that a ghost can manifest, there are many ways that we can detect or become aware of their presence. Often we see or hear things that we can't explain, but we still can't be one hundred percent certain that there was not a natural source. This is why it can take months, even years, to become convinced that your house is haunted.

A few incidents you couldn't debunk might be interesting and make you wonder, but if you have enough of these completely inexplicable instances over time, you might be more convinced. Liken it to a court of law: If the evidence presented is circumstantial, you may be suspicious of the guilt of the accused, but you need a preponderance of the evidence to be certain enough to convict.

Although there are many types of circumstantial symptoms, most hauntings have more than one of these over the years. When people tell me what's happening in their homes, one of the things I look for is multiple types of potential symptoms. Of course this isn't a hard-fast rule — some homes might only have one type of manifestation repeating consistently over time and yet are haunted. I just find that much more often than not, if there is a ghost hanging around, you will likely find a few of these symptoms sounding quite familiar.

SEEING IS BELIEVING

The Holy Grail for most ghost hunters is to see a full-bodied apparition. Still, this is a rather rare event for anyone. Many of us have been in this field for years without such a pleasure while others — those not even looking or wanting to see someone who is not bodily present — may happen upon such a sighting completely unexpectedly. For some reason that's how it usually goes.

To those who are lucky enough to see a full-bodied apparition, the spirit may appear perfectly solid and detailed, indistinguishable from the living…at least until it vanishes into thin air. Sometimes it's seen as a purely white being, or it may be colored but translucent, with objects behind it clearly visible. The sighting might be out of the corner of your eye or directly in front of you. It could be fleeting, gone so quickly that you wonder if it was really even there in the first place, or it may linger for a moment, even several minutes in rare cases.

If it is a residual energy, it will appear to be completely unaware of your presence. If you happen to be in its customary path, the apparition is likely to pass right through you — as if you are the one who does not exist.

Visual sightings don't always involve the entire body. Partial apparitions are almost as common as full ones. You might see a figure only from the waist up, from the waist down, or even just a leg or part of an arm and hand. In partial apparitions there doesn't appear to be significance to what part you see.

My son has seen the apparition of a cat in our house several times. At first it was only out of the corner of his eye, leaving him with a shadow of doubt after each sighting. Since we have several very live cats that are always on the prey, the doubt was even greater — until one evening he finally saw the mystery cat directly in front of him and watched it walk several feet before it faded from view. There was no doubt that this cat wasn't one of ours…or at least not one of our current ones. All four legs were invisible, but its back, head, and tail were present. The part he saw was as detailed as any living feline: A gray and brown tiger cat with white paws, to be exact, and it was completely transparent.

One other type of visual encounter is what is commonly referred to as "shadow people." These types of sightings are actually among the most common, although the variations are quite extensive. They range from wisps of shadows darting in dark corners or just at the edge of your vision, disappearing any time you turn to look, to clear and sharp-edged human sized shadows, mostly described as male and sometimes detailed enough to make out characteristics of clothing such as a hat, hood, or cape.

In between these extremes are softer-edged shadowy apparitions. Shadow people are often described as being the size of a small man or larger child, although this is not always the case.

Top: Mike captures a black shadow behind several bright orbs in the attic of our Cedar Run client.
Bottom: This photo, taken five seconds later, shows no such shadow — nor did any of the other shots taken that night. *Photos courtesy of Mike Pabian.*

In our home we have seen both a child-sized shadow person, always walking the same path, and an adult-sized vision in several different rooms.

One commonality amongst shadow people is their darkness. Although sometimes described in shades of gray, they are most often seen as the deepest of black, a darkness thicker than the night itself, so devoid of light that their outline is clear even in a darkened room. Shadow people may fade back into the shadows, disappear into walls, or dissolve right in front of you.

There are many theories on what shadow people are. Personally I believe that some are indeed simply ghosts or that ghosts, when manifesting, can do so (whether intentionally or not) as shadow people. Many of the houses I know to be haunted have had sightings of shadow people. The correlation between these sightings and other symptoms of being haunted is, for me, simply too strong to write off as coincidental. However, all shadow people may not be so neatly explained and there are many theories as to what they really are.

Dark clouds or shadowy mists are another type of sighting often thought to be paranormal. In my own experience, I have found these to be more common than I had originally expected, and so far seen only in places I believe to be haunted based on other evidence. They are often seen floating near the ceiling and typically appear as shapeless black masses that may drift before dissolving or disappearing altogether.

DID YOU HEAR THAT?

Disembodied Voices

A disembodied voice is just that — a voice we hear with our own ears that has no bodily source. Surprisingly they are not all that uncommon. You may hear your name called or barely audible whispers of nearby conversations when you're alone. If the voice is clear and audible, it is typically limited to a few brief words.

When a disembodied voice is heard during an investigation, it will usually be captured on the audio recording. Thus, if a voice is heard with someone's ears and also captured on a recording, it's noted as a disembodied voice and not an EVP.

Raps and Knockings

Rappings and knockings are the cornerstones of spirit manifestations. Maybe these are simply effects that are somehow the easiest for ghosts to achieve. No one knows for certain why many spirits gravitate towards this means of communication.

Incidents of rapping and knocking can be one-time events or might go on for years. Frequencies and durations can also vary. As with any other potentially paranormal phenomena, these types of incidents can have natural causes as well, thus a thorough debunking is warranted before jumping to any conclusions. Oftentimes in a haunting the knocking will be accompanied by other symptoms, but sometimes it's the only unexplainable activity. Loud knocking is one of the hallmarks of a poltergeist haunting, so if that is what you are experiencing you might want to do a little research about this special category of paranormal activity.

Scratching sounds are also commonly reported, especially in walls and ceilings. Naturally one's first thought is critters and, in many cases, that is indeed the explanation. The sounds could also be from an outside branch or another object blowing in the breeze. Scratching sounds are sometimes attributed to evil or demonic hauntings, but just because you have unexplainable scratching sounds does not mean you are experiencing a negative haunting. As with anything paranormal, the symptoms need to be considered as a whole to even hope to make sense of the situation.

Other Odd Sounds

The world of the paranormal is certainly filled with a myriad of sounds. In addition to voices, knocks, and scratching, the sounds of footsteps are fairly prevalent. They can be soft and subtle or loud and echoing. The sound of footsteps on stairs is also quite common — even when the stairs no longer exist.

Other often-heard sounds are those of doors, cabinets, and drawers opening and closing, unseen items being dropped, furniture being slid across the floor, balls being bounced, and music being played. If you hear the same sounds over and over again, there's a good chance they are simply residual. However, if upon hearing a door slam, you find a previously open door now closed with no logical explanation, if you hear footsteps and find footprints in the light coating of baby powder you sprinkled the night before, if the knocks you hear seem to respond to attempts to communicate, then you might be dealing with an intelligent haunting.

OTHER SENSES AT WORK

Being Touched

To feel a firm hand on your shoulder, to have your hair pulled, or to be otherwise touched by someone not physically present is by far one of the most unnerving and convincing ways of knowing your house is haunted. Other common experiences are feeling someone brush by you or being gently poked. The sensation of walking through cobwebs when none are around is also considered to be an encounter with a spirit or with the residue of one.

Often these types of encounters are fleeting, leaving you to wonder if they happened at all. You may find yourself going over the incident again and again in an attempt to make sense of it or be tempted to dismiss it altogether. However, when you know what you felt, and you are fairly sure you haven't lost your marbles, what it comes right down to is that something or someone touched you — yet did so without the benefit of a physical body.

Touches frequently come from crossed-over spirits, especially at a time when you are feeling down or could use some support. They can also come from earthbounds who simply want to make you aware of their presence. The two can often be distinguished by circumstance: If you're sitting quietly on your bed worrying about something and you feel an arm around your shoulder, chances are it is a loved one visiting to offer comfort. However, if you're washing the dishes and you feel a distinct tug on your shirt, it is likely an earthbound spirit messing with you.

Haunting Smells

The whiff of perfume, the scent of a cigar, the lingering smell of roses... These can all be associated with paranormal activity. Of course, they all can have perfectly natural explanations as well. Unexplained aromas are thought to be signs from those who have crossed-over

— gentle reminders that our loved ones are still with us in spirit.

Some smells are more likely to be residual in nature, such as when the scent of burning wood fills a room and then disappears just as quickly as it arrived. Perhaps a house formerly on the property burned down or maybe the site was used for ceremonial campfires or cremations in years gone by.

I NEED SOME ZZZs

Sleep Paralysis and Old Hags

Sleep paralysis is the term given to the experience of waking up fully conscious but unable to move your trunk and limbs. You often feel as if a heavy weight is on your chest or that it's difficult to breathe. You may try to scream, but no sound comes out. These incidents can last from only a few seconds to several minutes, longer in rare cases, and are often accompanied by hallucinations of intruders, shadows, voices, smells, or feeling as if you're levitating. Almost always they leave the victim with the feeling of terror or an evil presence.

Although these are truly frightening experiences, they are also a natural phenomena. When the brain goes into a cycle of REM (rapid eye movement) sleep, it prepares for this dream state by relaxing the body. This helps prevent your dreaming actions from translating into physical movements. If you awaken during this transitional period, you are likely to be fully conscious yet your brain is not able to control your body. The hallucinations are a side-effect of the transition between a dream state and consciousness, although they feel perfectly real at the time.

It's not at all surprising that throughout history this experience has been associated with various negative paranormal explanations, many of which persist even though science now better understands the natural reasons for its occurrence. Various cultures have different names for the experience and different stories to go along with it as well. One of the most common is "Old Hag Syndrome," alluding to the theory that a witch or "old hag" has crept upon your chest, rendering you immobile.

Even though sleep paralysis is very frightening, it is generally not considered to be a sign of a serious condition and is actually fairly common. It often happens when a person's normal sleep patterns have been impacted by travel, stress, shift changes, or other factors.

Although the vast majority of sleep paralysis episodes are perfectly normal, some are indeed associated with a haunting. Telling the difference is not easy. I tend to believe such episodes are due to natural causes unless I hear of other extenuating circumstances or collaborating evidence. For example, if you suddenly experience sleep paralysis at the same time that someone else in the home has a significant paranormal experience, then there might be more to it. Also, if multiple people in the home suddenly begin experiencing the phenomena and sleep schedules have been disrupted, or if the house has other symptoms of a haunting, I'd be hard pressed not to consider it potentially paranormal.

Recurring Nightmares

A nightmare is a realistic disturbing dream that often awakens you from a deep sleep, leaving you uneasy if not frightened. As with sleep paralysis, they are a common natural occurrence. They happen more frequently in children, but still torment adults at times. Many things are thought to have a hand in triggering nightmares, including late-night snacks, medications, substance withdrawal, and even certain sleep disorders.

Can spirits also invade your dreams and cause nightmares? Yes, I believe they can. In homes I know to be haunted, the homeowners have had significant nightmares that I truly believe to have been seeded by the earthbound entities with which they share their homes. It's difficult to distinguish normal nightmares from those that might be triggered by an earthbound spirit, but if nightmares are unusual for you and they are accompanied by other paranormal activity in the home, they may indeed be related.

OTHER SYMPTOMS OF HAUNTINGS

Being Watched

Above and beyond the five senses, sometimes we notice a spirit's presence in other ways. The most common is the feeling of being watched. This sensation can occur naturally in some people as a side-effect of high EMF levels. EMF is energy with wave frequencies below 300 hertz or cycles per second. Our daily lives are full of constant exposure to these man-made fields in varying intensities. Outside the home they are caused by power lines and microwave towers. Inside they are created by electronic devices such as televisions, computer screens, fluorescent lights, microwave ovens, cell phones, and clock radios. The wiring of your home also gives off EMF. If there is an area in your home where you feel as if someone is always watching you, a sensation especially common in basements where higher EMF levels occur, that's all it might be. Other side-effects include

headaches, dizziness, and paranoia. Some individuals are more sensitive to high EMF levels than others.

If you are experiencing any of these feelings, especially if they happen only in a particular area of the house, you should consider checking the EMF levels in that area. Sometimes, however, the feeling of being watched isn't due to high EMF or any other natural cause. Sometimes we really are being watched — just not by someone still among the living.

Odd Emotions

Empathy is the ability to perceive the emotions or feelings of others. Some people are especially empathetic and those with a strong ability are generally known as "Empaths." As with any psychic ability, many people have this gift to a lesser degree. Some Empaths are in tune with the feelings of the living while others seem to be more impacted by impressions from the dead.

Spirits sometimes project their emotions or feelings as a method of communication. Those with stronger empathetic abilities can be more susceptible to this type of communication, but anyone may experience this at one time or another. Generally these encounters can be recognized by a sudden and overpowering feeling such as sadness that seems to have no logical explanation. Usually the feeling passes as quickly as it comes on, but for those with heightened sensitivities it may linger a bit longer or be difficult to shake off.

Electronics

One of the most common ways spirits choose to show themselves is through the manipulation of electronics. Often it's as simple as a light or television coming on by itself or batteries in the smoke alarms being drained on a regular basis. Even iPods® and cellular phones have been known to become play toys for the dead. For many spirits the ability to manipulate electronics seems to come quite naturally, and that may make perfect sense. After all, they are themselves purely energy.

Pets

Pets can be one of the best barometers when it comes to sensing paranormal activity. Dogs may bark and stare as if watching something we ourselves can't see, often taking a guarding stance. Or they may refuse to enter a certain room or area of the house or cower, whimper or whine with no apparent reason. Cats may be entertained or intrigued by something unseen by human eyes. Animals have sharper senses and psychic abilities then humans do. Pay attention to what they notice.

Pets have heightened sensitivity to paranormal activity. *Photo courtesy of Debbie McGee.*

Doors, Cabinets, and Drawers Opening and Closing

Another classic symptom of a haunting is the opening and closing of doors, cabinets, and drawers. Usually this will happen while no one is there to witness the event. The first few times you will likely think it was nothing or that someone must have inadvertently left the door or drawer open, but when it happens too often you may truly begin to wonder. For some reason kitchen cabinets tend to be a favorite ghostly playground, especially during overnight hours.

With poltergeists, this phenomenon, as with many others, may be amplified. Many people, myself included, report walking into a kitchen to find every single door and drawer open, as if a burglar had been frantically searching for valuables yet has left the cabinet contents completely untouched.

Items Disappearing and Reappearing

Another favorite trick of ghosts and poltergeists alike is to "borrow" regularly used items. Keys are notorious for disappearing, as are personal items such as glasses, watches, jewelry, and even shoes. Really, it might be anything, but most often it's something you're likely to be looking for, or possibly something you've recently touched.

The items might only stay missing for a few hours, but often it's days, sometimes even weeks. When they do reappear, it is usually exactly where you left them, but sometimes just the opposite is true — you'll find them someplace completely unexpected such as on top of the refrigerator or in the middle of the bath tub. If this happens, your ghost is likely just having some fun or trying to get your attention. Of course, if you need the missing item for something important like getting to work, it can be quite annoying and at times downright aggravating. Most people prefer not to call their boss and explain that their ghost hid their car keys yet again.

Sometimes you might be successful in having an item returned by simply asking. When something goes missing, first walk a short distance from the room where the object had been (in other words, give the ghost a little privacy) and then, in a firm but unemotional tone, say something along the lines of "Hey there. I know you took my keys. Ha ha — cute trick. But now I really need to go to work so please put them back where you found them." Give it a few minutes, and then see if you have had any luck. If that doesn't work, a slightly stronger version might do the trick.

Imaginary Friends

Children have imaginary friends all the time, and most often it isn't anything paranormal. Still, if the friend is more then a passing fancy you may want to do a little investigating to be sure. Start by listening in on your child's play time. If they have conversations with the imaginary friend, does your child pause to let her friend answer, or do they answer for them? If it's the latter, the friend is probably indeed imaginary. If not, some further sleuthing may be in order. Of course if you actually hear another voice responding, then that's a whole different story...

Next, listen to the types of conversations your child and their "friend" are having. Are they appropriate for your child's age? Is the information shared limited to things you would expect your child to know? Finally, ask your child what their friend says to them. If they are telling your child to do bad things or cause harm to themselves or others, or if they caution them not to let mommy or daddy know what they talk about, then your concerns may be well-founded.

Another clue to a not-so-imaginary friendship is if a younger child casually announces that their friend is dead and there has been no recent exposure to death or the concept. Also, if your child indicates that their friend is angry at them or has been hostile in any way, or your child reports that their friend isn't another child but someone older or possibly scary looking, you should be concerned.

It is not uncommon for spirits to befriend children as they are more likely to be open to communication than adults. Often a ghost acquaintance may not be problematic, but occasionally the spirit may have a different agenda then simple friendship. If you suspect your child's friend is less then imaginary and you see any red flags in the relationship I recommend seeking the help of a paranormal professional.

Of course, if a child is talking about hurting themselves or anyone else, instead of simply assuming their imaginary friend isn't all that imaginary after all please seriously consider seeking professional counseling as well.

Physical Assault

Scratches, slaps, and hard shoves — any physical encounter more serious than a firm touch — can be quite disturbing. Fortunately, this type of interaction is quite rare. Unfortunately, it can sometimes, but not always, be a sign of a demonic or non-human presence.

More significantly, ghosts have been accused of doing more serious bodily harm by such acts as pushing someone down a flight of stairs. Just as some people in life can be quite nasty, so can some ghosts. If you are experiencing anything that has you frightened or concerned in any way, you might want to contact someone experienced in the field to help you better understand your situation and your options.

Mechanical and Other Home Maintenance Issues

Sometimes a spirit will take great pleasure in messing with the mechanics of your home. You may find appliances starting to have issues or ceasing to function altogether. Water heaters may stop heating water or furnaces and air-conditioning units may go on the fritz. One of my clients lost three televisions in a matter of months. If you are having more than your fair share of home maintenance issues, or if you have ever wondered if you might have gremlins, you might consider the possibility that the cause is an active haunting instead.

Quarreling and Relationship Issues

Whether this happens as the direct intent of a spirit trying to stir up a little emotional energy, or simply because tensions and relationships are stressed because of lack of sleep or other issues related to a haunting, the result is the same. If you have considered the fact that your house may indeed be haunted and you notice increased quarreling, especially while in the home, there may be a correlation. By simply acknowledging this and avoiding any quarreling for a while, you may be able to quell some of the activity.

Moving or Levitating Objects

Doors slamming forcefully, objects flying off shelves, pictures jumping off walls, or just about anything floating in mid-air is often the sign of a significant haunting, if not a poltergeist. Although certain plumbing configurations or issues make it more likely that a faucet can turn on by itself, this phenomena is also sometimes caused by resident spirits.

Hot and Cold Spots

If certain areas of your home often seem to be unexpectedly warmer or colder than the surrounding areas with no discernible cause, this might potentially be a symptom of a ghostly presence. Cold areas are much more prevalent then warm spots. Warm areas are thought by some to be symptomatic of negative entities, but I have known them to occur in non-negative hauntings as well.

Cold spots can affect people as well as rooms. Sometimes they start and end quickly or seem to pass right through you, while other times they linger briefly. You may feel one over your entire body or only on a specific area. In some haunted homes a particular room in the house will always be colder than the rest with no logical explanation. One theory is that spirits, especially if they are trying to manifest, draw energy from the environment leaving the area significantly chillier.

Other Physical Evidence

Unexplained hand- or footprints, writing on paper or walls, objects found piled or stacked in the middle of the room or in unusual ways all can be indications of an active spirit. Although these types of manifestations are less common, ghosts have been known to be quite creative.

Debunking

The interpretation of haunting symptoms can be distorted by expectations. Most people move into a home without any thought that it might be haunted. Symptoms may persist for months or even years unnoticed or ignored. However once you begin to wonder if your house is haunted, you will likely view the same events quite differently. Suddenly every little sound or shadow is noticed, assessed, and considered potentially paranormal.

It's always important to rule out natural causes for any potentially paranormal event. Many of the haunting symptoms we've discussed are caused by something easily explained. Even if you're convinced that your house is haunted, or especially if you're convinced it's haunted, you should make a habit of trying to debunk everything that strikes you as a ghostly manifestation. Here you will find some things to keep in mind as you're doing so.

Creepy Critters

Mice, squirrels, chipmunks, raccoons, bats, and even cats are notorious for finding their way into attics and crawl spaces. They can cause scratching sounds, bumps, knocks, even sounds that could be interpreted as the cries of a baby or child. One simple trick for telling if the noises coming from a particular area are due to a live creature of one sort or another is to sprinkle a light coating of baby powder and check the next day for little paw prints. Fresh droppings in an area are also a sure sign that critters are present.

When the Wind Blows

Another common cause of worrisome sounds are small openings that might let in a little wind — and a little wind can make a lot of noise. These small cracks and crevices can also cause cold spots. One trick here is to light a candle and move it slowly around the walls or windows where a breeze may be coming through, being careful not to catch anything on fire, of course. Draft detector tools are also available and quite a bit safer. Use masking tape as a temporary solution for any small holes or cracks you might find. Often the smallest of cracks can create significant haunted house sound effects on a windy night.

Plumb Scary

Another common source of deceitfully scary noises is the pipes or air ducts within a home. Pipes can be the source of sounds similar to moaning and groaning as well as knocking, especially with radiators or hot water baseboard heat when a little air gets in the pipes or when they are expanding or contracting with temperature changes. Loose brackets can cause a loud rattling type of knocking when a system turns on or off creating pressure changes.

High EMF

High EMF can be the source of feelings of paranoia or of being watched. If you don't happen to have an EMF meter or a friend from whom to borrow one, try purchasing a cheap compass, even a child's toy version, at your local discount store. First use the compass to identify north, the direction the needle will be pointing when the device is held still. Then move the compass to various locations around the room, giving it time to settle in each spot. If the needle spins or rocks continually, or settles into pointing to a different direction as north, you have likely found a source of EMF. If you move a foot or two away from the source, the compass should return to normal. The further away from the source you need to get before the aberrant behavior stops, the stronger the EMF field. A paranormal investigation team should be equipped with an EMF meter and can assist you in identifying whether high EMF levels are an issue in your home.

Fun with Electronics

Lights, televisions, ceiling fans, and other devices turning on and off are often cited as evidence of a potential haunting. However, in a world of both radio frequency (RF) and infrared (IR) remote controls, these occurrences can often be logically explained. IR remote controls require a clear line of sight to the receiving device and their range typically extends about thirty feet while RF remote controls can go through walls and around corners with a range of roughly one hundred feet.

Your neighbor could be inadvertently affecting something in your home controlled by an RF remote. Devices controlled by IR are usually only affected by IR remotes within the home, though an IR remote control could be affecting other devices within its line of sight. Mirrors may also reflect the signals of the remotes, often sending them in unexpected directions.

Medication Side Effects

Many medications, especially prescribed drugs, can have unusual side effects that may cause a person's perception to be somewhat distorted. If you have any concerns, speak to your doctor. You might also want to ask others in the household if they have shared your experiences. If so, you may be able to rule medication side effects out as a likely cause. Or, if you're hearing sounds you can't explain, put out a recorder when the sounds are most likely to be heard and see if you can capture evidence that might disprove side effects as a potential cause. However, please limit your recording attempts as noted in Chapter 6.

Chapter Four

Why Are Ghosts Here?

---

*"Some places speak distinctly. Certain dank gardens
cry aloud for a murder; certain old houses demand to be
haunted; certain coasts are set apart for shipwrecks."*

— *Robert Louis Stevenson*

What in the world are ghosts and spirits doing on our earthly plane anyway? Shouldn't they be in the great here-after doing whatever it is spirits do over there? If they aren't, if somehow they are here with us, exactly why is that and how did it happen? To answer such questions, we need to again differentiate between crossed-over and earthbound spirits as they are each here for very different reasons.

Let's begin with crossed-over spirits. I believe they're actually around us much more often than we may be aware, but the signs they give us of their presence are certainly not a daily occurrence. How do crossed-over spirits communicate with us? With them, it's usually the small things: a whiff of their perfume or cigar, a song on the radio, or a flower that catches our eye in an unusual way. Sometimes signs come in multiples, such as hearing their name three times in the same afternoon. In fact, any reminder of them repeated in a brief period of time may be a sign of their presence.

A sign could also be something as simple as a bird, an animal, or a rainbow, especially one that appears just after thinking or speaking of your loved one, or that seems out of place, like a single bloom of a cut flower found along your path.

Sometimes their communication is a bit more direct. An item of theirs, jewelry, perhaps, may be found sitting out on the dresser when you're certain it was previously tucked away. Their favorite chair may be spotted gently rocking away. You may feel a comforting arm around you in a time of need. Or you may even see them, most frequently joining you briefly in everyday situations such as while driving, mowing the yard, or even shopping. One theory for these casual drop-ins is that they want us to realize their visit isn't anything unusual — they're often with us, day-to-day, as we live our lives.

Crossed-over spirits often visit us in our dreams. Normal dreams are usually disjointed, distorted, and morphing versions of reality that are anything but clear in their message, if there is one at all. Visitation dreams are much more realistic and straightforward, with the conversation, and thus the message, easily understood.

I have an Australian friend, Melissa, who believes that those who have passed can and do communicate with us through our dreams. In fact, she's had several such experiences herself. Melissa feels that crossed-over spirits may come through to us to let us know they are now at peace or to share with the family that they are no longer suffering.

She recently had such a visitation from her mum's partner, Peter, who had just committed suicide. In her dream she and Peter stood on either side of a big wooden table. On it he showed her a stack of jigsaw pieces. Each represented something or someone. One piece was her mum, another was his son. Two more were her mum's family and the house that he and her mum had just brought.

As Melissa stood watching the table, Peter started shuffling the pieces and mixing them around. He told her that this was how his mind was — his thoughts were jumbled and he wasn't thinking straight and couldn't put the pieces of the puzzle together. Then a feeling came over her of spinning around really fast in a circle, not being able to see anything clearly or keep her balance.

With the dream Melissa was given a better understanding of why Peter chose to take his own life and she was able to share this with her mum. Often in a time of loss spirits seem to find it easier to offer messages to loved ones though others. The pain of the recent loss often blocks direct contact to those whom they are closest.

No matter how a crossed-over spirit comes to visit, it will do so with the intent of offering something, be it support, information, or simply peace of mind. Earthbound spirits, on the other hand, have an entirely different agenda and their methods of communication can be just as different. They can also visit in dreams, but the dreams will be more convoluted or even nightmares.

Earthbound spirits can also communicate with us in many ways. They can knock, bang, turn on electronics, even open and close doors, but mostly it's for their own benefit, not yours. Many believe they do the things they do simply to get our attention — to let us know they're there. Can you imagine what it would be like living in a world where your very existence was unnoticed by anyone? You too might well do anything and everything you could simply to be acknowledged. Some believe that ghostly manifestations are meant to invoke emotion in the living, and that this emotional energy is a sort of a food source for them. After all they are purely energy.

WHY THEY DIDN'T CROSS OVER

For all the Earthbound spirits roaming the earth, several questions abound. Why are they here? Why didn't they cross over when they had the chance? Can they go any time they like?

While we might never know the answers to these questions, one of our best sources for such information is mediums. These gifted individuals have been given the ability to communicate in one form or another with those who have died. Some mediums, such as John Edward, are able to communicate with, and receive messages from, spirits that have crossed over. Other mediums, such as Mary Ann Winkowski, profess to be able to see and converse *only* with earthbound spirits.

One of the most commonly recognized types of earthbound spirits is those whose death was sudden, unexpected, or otherwise tragic. This little tidbit isn't one we needed to learn from mediums; it's simply a trend that was noted centuries ago. Where there has been an untimely death, there is a greater chance of a haunting. Why is that? One theory is that their demise happened so quickly that they never quite realized, or perhaps refused to accept, that they were dead. Think about it: One minute you are driving down the highway mentally assembling your grocery list; the next you're wandering by the roadside, interrupted by some horrible car accident with the mangled wreckage right in front of you. You need to go... after all, you have things to do and people are expecting you. Yet somehow everything is unclear, misty, convoluted — and for some reason no one will speak to you. They're all too busy with the poor victims of that horrid accident. No matter, you're not far from home. You'll just walk...

Another theory is that a sudden death is simply difficult to come to terms with. Our spirits get quite attached to the bodies we occupy while on this planet, the lives we live here, and the people we come to love. Leaving all that behind to return to the spirit world with little or no notice can be a bit much for some. Given the choice between a grand hereafter and a little more time on earth, minus the little detail of having a body, they choose to remain close to their earthly life, possessions, and loved ones.

As a variation of that, it's possible that upon death spirits are simply confused. Who wouldn't be? A sudden transition from thinking with one's brain to thinking without any brain at all may not be all that easy. Maybe some of them don't mean to stay. Maybe, as many mediums believe, there's a brief window of opportunity where we can remain here and adjust to the transition, attend our own funeral services, and then go peacefully into the light.

Perhaps some spirits just get confused somewhere along the way and miss that window of opportunity. Maybe as time passes after the death of the body everything becomes more and more muddled and confused. Thus they become stuck, earthbound, wandering through their home wondering who the strange new people who have moved in are and trying desperately to let them know that they are still there.

Another reason a spirit may choose not to cross over is the age-old theme of unfinished business. It might be something important to them in life or an issue involving the wellbeing of their family. It could be that they never mentioned to their wife that they stashed a lifetime of savings beneath the floorboards in the dining room and they just intend to stay long enough to get their message across. Their reason could also be something more sinister — maybe they were murdered and they simply cannot rest until justice has been served or vengeance delivered.

Fear can be another reason for earthbounds deciding not to cross over. Some may have committed heinous acts in their lifetime and now fear getting their comeuppance for those deeds. Others may have committed suicide and fear the consequences of that final choice. Children may worry that they did something wrong that caused their death in the first place, especially if it also resulted in the death of others.

One of the sadder theories about why spirits sometimes stay behind is because those who loved them cannot let them go. They see the pain and sadness their spouses, children, or parents are going through and they hope that by staying they can lessen that pain. Perhaps loved ones even beg them not to go, to stay with them in whatever way they can, and they concede to do so. They may intend this to be temporary — only to find themselves many years later earthbound and alone.

These scenarios give rise to another question: Can they cross over whenever they want? This is one topic that I have found no clear answer on. Some people believe they cannot, that the light, portal, or tunnel only remains for a short period after our death, generally fading after our funeral. However, most believe that spirits can cross at any time, although they might require help to do so.

We will talk a bit more about helping spirits cross over, sometimes referred to as Spirit Rescue, in a later chapter. I personally believe that once a spirit has been around for a while they may become confused or their perceptions distorted and talking to them can help clarify things for them. One of the most common EVPs we capture is simply the word "Help." We may not have all the answers, but I believe when they ask for help we must do our best to try.

WHERE DO THEY COME FROM?

Visiting crossed-over spirits are not found in any particular location. They can come to us wherever we are, but what about the earthbound spirits? We certainly might expect to find them in the home they spent their life and final days in, or in the location at which they passed, especially if their death was a suicide, murder, or otherwise tragic.

If you're convinced that your house is haunted, does that mean someone died there? What if the home is fairly new and you're the first owners or you have lived in the home for many years in complete peace and quiet and suddenly things are starting to go bump in the night? Where did your invisible roommates come from?

First, it's fairly well accepted amongst mediums and paranormal researchers that earthbound spirits are not bound to any particular location — they can go where they want whenever they want simply, some believe, by thinking about it. This certainly fits with everything I have seen in terms of hauntings, but it doesn't necessarily explain just why one might wander into your house and want to stay. (We'll discuss "What would make it want to go back where it came from?" a little later…)

From the Land

One reason a ghost might be hanging around in a newer home is that they became attached to the land long before the house was built. I hear a lot of people with hauntings theorize that maybe their residence was built on an old Indian burial ground. Perhaps, but probably not. More typically a spirit was attached to a home previously on the property or nearby — or perhaps a traveler met an ill-fated demise in the area in days gone by. Still, the presence of the spirit of Indians is quite possible, even if you aren't living on top of their burial grounds.

Maria, who we will meet in a later chapter, discovered this candleholder while digging in the garden. Could a spirit possibly have come inside with it? *Photo courtesy of Debbie McGee.*

Haunted Objects

Sometimes a ghost will be attached to an object. I would venture to guess that for these spirits there must be some reason that hanging out at home just isn't so appealing. Maybe they needed a break from their spouse, or possibly the new owners just drive them a little crazy or they can't stand their décor. In any case, for whatever reason, ghosts sometimes follow an object instead of hanging out at home.

Any object can have an attachment, but generally it will be something treasured during the spirit's lifetime: jewelry, silverware, furniture, large mirrors, portraits, dolls, and even cars have all been known to be haunted. If an object is old and you don't know its history, you might be getting more than you bargained for with its purchase.

Granted, if you're just an occasional purchaser of used or antique items, the likelihood of bringing home something

In the workshop at Empire Antiques, the treasures of those who have passed are brought back to life. It was in this location that my team had an interesting flashlight conversation with a male spirit who indicated he was there because of his belongings.

with its former owner in tow is quite low. On the other hand, if you make a lot of such purchases or have a house full of antiques and find yourself living with uninvited guests, then consider this as a possible source.

However, that's not to say you shouldn't purchase anything previously owned without knowing its history. Just pay a little more attention when doing so if you're concerned. If you feel both drawn to an object but also get a bit of a bad feeling about it at the same time, you might want to reconsider the purchase — and if the shopkeeper mentions that the item has a bad history to it, or even outright claims that it's haunted, you are best to walk away empty-handed.

One of my favorite paranormal investigations was at Empire Antiques, a 75,000-square-foot, two-story warehouse in Hightstown, New Jersey. The owner, Gene Pascucci, has been buying antiques and estates up and down the East Coast for decades and has had furniture shipped in from Italy and Egypt as well. His store is a melding of the memories and treasures of many lives, and it seems that some lost spirits have chosen not to leave those memories behind. My team had originally been called in to investigate Gene's home by his wife, Kathy. One spirit there was believed to be a previous owner, an elderly woman named Mrs. Carr, but there were signs of other spirits as well. With all of the beautiful antiques in the home, that wasn't too surprising.

If you have lived in a house for years with no hints of a disembodied roommate and suddenly unusual things begin to happen, do a quick time line. Speak to everyone in the house and see when the activity really started. Look at what changed just before then. If an antique or older object was brought into the home at the time, you may want to consider asking a friend to let you store it in their attic or garage for a bit just to see if the activity ceases. Of course if your friend then starts having a bit of activity, they may be dropping it back on your doorstep pronto, but at least you'll know.

If you do find yourself with a haunted object, you shouldn't burn or destroy it. Instead contact someone with experience in handling such items.

Attachments to People

Spirits may become attached to people just as easily as they might to an object. I'm not talking about a physical type of attachment, although that certainly can happen. A spirit "attachment" is often just a ghost who has decided they like hanging out with someone for whatever reason. There might just be something about that person that they relate to or maybe they're an old friend or relative. In such cases, moving to a different home isn't going to solve anything.

Attachments frequently happen to those psychically sensitive or people with a heightened awareness to the energy of spirits. It's possible that ghosts just feel like they have a better chance of communicating with such people or that these gifted individuals give off a different type of energy than the rest of us. Many people may not even realize they have such sensitivities.

Keep in mind that crossed-over spirits don't attach to people — they simply visit. The concept only applies to earthbound spirits.

Tagalongs

If you go to enough haunted places, something's bound to follow you home sooner or later. Even if you don't realize that somewhere you've been is haunted, you might still bring home a tagalong, also commonly known as a hitchhiker. Ghosts need vacations, too, and if you interest them for any reason they may follow you home, invitation or not. And apparently ghosts often find paranormal investigators quite interesting.

The good news about tagalongs is that they rarely unpack their bags and take up permanent residence. Typically they'll just make themselves at home for a few days, a few weeks at most. Of course, as with any house guest, some are more difficult to get rid of than others. Most paranormal investigators have their own personal routines for preventing tagalongs before leaving potentially haunted locations. Usually these involve prayer, verbally (and firmly) letting them know they aren't welcome, energy work, or a combination of all three.

When I first started as a ghost hunter, I was well practiced in doing my tagalong prevention routine after nighttime investigations, but somehow I didn't even think about it when I first visited a client during the day. Even after the initial visit to this particular house, I was suspicious that something paranormal was going on there. For one thing, the homeowners had mentioned hearing music when none was being played. While listening to the recordings of our conversations that evening, some unusual music faded in and out, although none was playing during my visit.

Once back home, a few issues popping up with my computer made me take notice and wonder — they were just little annoying things, but enough to make me suspicious. A few nights later I was with my family in the living room when we all heard some similarly odd music playing, briefly but loudly, from an adjacent room. It wasn't anything that any of us had heard before, and not a sound made by any electronic device we owned. Luckily I happen to have a very patient and supportive family. No one freaked out and the only comment I got was along the lines of "Bringing home stray dogs and stray cats is one thing, but you need to draw the line at bringing home stray ghosts."

Wandering Children

I have heard many times that children's spirits may wander from home to home to find other children. I can't say for certain that this is true, but I tend to believe it. Children spirits might not have the attachment to physical places or objects that an adult spirit does. Initially they might prefer to stay with family, but what of when the family is gone? It's not unreasonable to think the child's ghost might wander the neighborhood a bit looking for other children, possibly seeking a playmate that can see or hear them, one who is open to an "imaginary" friend. When that child outgrows them, or simply can't see or hear them any longer, they might wander down the road to find the next little girl or boy to play with.

One possibility with a roaming child spirit is that they might find someone with maternal qualities. If so, maybe they stick around for a little while and try to get the woman's attention. If that works and if they can somehow let the woman know they're there, then that might be the closest thing they've had to a mother in a very long time and they might decide to stay. This scenario is certainly a possibility in the Cedar Run case we will be discussing in Chapter 10.

To sum up, if your children have suddenly discovered an imaginary friend and other symptoms of a haunting have begun as well, then maybe a lost and lonely child has chosen your family as a temporary refuge. If so, you might want to consider letting them stay or better yet offer them help in crossing over. I find the spirits of children to be the most heartbreaking. They can sound happy and playful in some of the EVPs yet ask for help in others — and if any spirit deserves to be helped instead of thrown into the streets, it is that of a child.

Through the Portal

There are a lot of theories about portals — how they are opened, what they are, and who might come through. Many people feel that mirrors can be portals and, while I don't doubt that can sometimes be true, not every mirror is a portal. Some people swear that a closet in their home is a portal. More likely, if something odd is going on, they are sensing a spirit's hiding spot. Still, they could be right.

Séances can open portals — and that's exactly what they're intended to do. If you know what you are doing and are strong in your energy work, you should be able to conduct a séance safely, with full control of who comes through and who doesn't. You also need to make sure they return to wherever they came from and the doorway has been closed before you conclude. If you aren't well trained in this art by someone with significant experience, I would strongly recommend you simply don't try it.

Ouija Boards are another commonly abused spirit communication tool that can open portals. Pretty much the same issues and rules apply here as for séances. I used to think the fear of Ouija Boards was just a lot of nonsense, but the more I learn the more convinced I am that they can be much more dangerous than they can be fun. You probably wouldn't open your front door in the middle of the night, plop down on the sofa, and call out for strangers passing by to come on in, would you? Well, that's just what you would be doing with an Ouija Board.

Nosey Neighbors

Another likely source for an occasional spirit dropping by is your neighbors. If your neighbor's house is haunted, you'll probably never know, but once in a while a spirit may stop by. If you live next to a funeral home or a cemetery, however, you may get a visit or two from those waiting to cross over. I doubt it would happen that often — I would be curious to know actually — but I would also be surprised if nothing odd ever happened.

Neighboring drop-bys might also be more common if you live next to one of the types of locations where spirits are often found: bars, theaters, hospitals, gyms, or anyplace where there is a constant stream of emotional energy. If you live next door to such a place, you may be subject to an occasional visit.

EMF Feasts

We have talked about how EMF is a by-product of man-made electrical sources and how higher than normal levels can cause feelings such as paranoia or being watched. In later chapters, we will discuss how spikes in EMF levels where there's no natural explanation can indicate spirit activity. However, locations with abnormally high EMF can have one more issue — they can become a feeding source for spirit activity.

Think of it this way: Spirits are energy and they seem to need energy to manifest. If the wiring in your home is old, or you have some other irregularity that causes large areas of high EMF, you may just be fueling the fire, so to speak. In ghost hunting we sometimes even create high energy areas with a device called an EMF pump. It's kind of like chumming: 'Yum, yum, come and get it! Would you mind telling me how you died while you're here?'

If you do have a home with unusually high EMF levels, you might also be tempting any potential visiting spirits to stay. It's not much different than if a stray dog followed you home and you fed it a nice steak dinner every night. For some spirits that might be all they need to decide to call your place home.

Negative Energy Manifestations

Some people believe that a build-up of negative energy itself can create paranormal activity. This is especially true in an environment with clutter or one that's dirty or unkempt. I truly believe the mind can create much more than we currently realize, both positive and negative. Our energy itself seems to affect the environment around us, even lingering after we've left the room, especially in the case of intense emotions.

Fights, stress, alcoholism, drug addiction, abuse, anything that can cause a negative emotional environment can have a lingering effect on the location. If the place is also cluttered or just generally grimy, another source of negativity, this energy can gather in the dusty nooks and crannies. In extreme circumstances, it may even take on a life of its own.

OTHER REASONS THINGS SUDDENLY START

One of the more frequent questions I get is: Why would a haunting suddenly begin after the family has lived peacefully and ghost-free for years? As we've already seen, spirits can drop in from anywhere at any time. More often than not, though, the spirit was probably there the whole time. It may have been quiet, preferring to keep to itself, or it may have lacked the energy to manifest to the point where you'd really take notice.

If you do find yourself with some activity that seems to have started suddenly, take a little time to think back. Discuss it with your family or anyone who has spent significant time in your home. Even talk to the previous owners if they happen to be available. You may find that little things have actually been going on all along and what you've noticed recently is simply an increase in the activity. If so, what would cause a typically quiet ghost to suddenly start causing a ruckus?

The most common reason is construction — any major remodeling or renovations will likely stir things up if anything is there to be stirred. The prevailing theory is that they were quite happy with their environment the way it was, thank you very much. Start tearing down their walls, ripping off their treasured wallpaper, changing things in any significant way, and you will likely have succeeded in making them at least a little upset.

Another theory is that the physical effort involved in a renovation might simply be feeding a resident spirit, allowing it more flexibility in manifesting. With a renovation the environment itself has had a sudden inoculation of the energy associated with physical labor. Even the hammering might be a contributing factor — there's a lot of energy being transferred from either man or nail gun into the very structure of the house itself.

Increases in paranormal activity during construction or remodeling are actually quite common. The good news is that this type of activity may be relatively short-lived. If all goes well, things should start to calm down a few weeks to a few months after the renovations are completed. Okay, for some people that may be way too long, but at least it's likely that things will eventually get better.

Another change that may increase the level of activity in a home is the onset of adolescence, even early adolescence, in one of the children in the home. Even if other children have already gone through this stage with no noticeable impact on the levels of paranormal activity, one particular child may suddenly have an effect.

We don't understand why this happens, but the answer may well be related to how poltergeist activity is often associated with adolescents and pre-adolescents, especially girls. During this stage of life the brain changes, undergoing an intense overproduction of gray matter in the frontal lobe. Poltergeist activity has been correlated with seizures, epilepsy, or other disturbances of the central nervous system, so it's not too far of a stretch to wonder if the physical changes a brain undergoes during adolescence might also come into play.

Often with hauntings the source of the spirit is as much a mystery as the activity itself. Sometimes, though, with a little homework and investigation the pieces will begin to come together. I have found that simply knowing a little something about who you're sharing your home with often helps lessen any anxiety of a haunting.

Psychic Children

If one of your children has been seeing spirits or sensing their presence, it is quite possible that the issue at hand isn't that your house is haunted, but that you have a psychic child. To differentiate, you will want to pay attention to see if others are noticing any symptoms of a haunting or if the experiences are limited to those of the child. Even so, it can be difficult to tell if the child is simply aware of a spirit in your home or if they have some degree of psychic abilities (or both!).

One young teenager I know showed signs of psychic ability as a toddler, but it faded (or was at least unnoticed by others) until he hit preadolescence, at which time he began to notice orbs, shadow people, and even full-bodied apparitions in his own home (yes, his home is haunted!). When his mother took him on a tour of historic locations, he had further experiences. Some of the energies he was picking up may have been residual in nature. He has occasionally displayed empathetic traits and has had success at animal communication. Sometimes he even sees the spirits of past pets.

Determining if your child has psychic abilities is well beyond the scope of this book. I would highly recommend Chip Coffey's *Growing Up Psychic: My Story of Not Just Surviving but Thriving – and How Others Like Me Can Too* for those who think they have a psychic child. Raising a child with psychic sensitivities can have its challenges. Chip Coffey offers some suggestions for the parents of psychic children:

- *Reassure and support your specially gifted psychic kids.*

- *Seek appropriate medical and/or psychiatric help to be certain there is no underlying physical or emotional problem.*

- *If your child is generally truthful, assume that he is also being truthful about his psychic experiences.*

- *Do your own homework and validate what your child is telling you.*

- *Don't let anyone misdiagnose or medicate your child for a mental illness he doesn't have.*

- *Don't let your desire to have a "special" child lead you to "see" abilities that aren't there- wishing doesn't make it so.*

- *Don't thrust your own fears of the paranormal upon your child.*

Chapter 5

Living with Ghosts

"Do you believe in ghosts?" asked a gentleman of Madame du Deffand. "No," replied the witty lady; "but I am afraid of them."

— Charles Harper, Haunted Houses (1907)

We all have our own unique and individual belief systems. They encompass everything from religion and life after death to the fundamentals of human nature. For a large part we believe what we are taught while growing up. By school age most children can discern fiction from reality, either in bedtime stories or on television. By the time we pass adolescence our views of reality have become fairly well rooted and are somewhat resistant to change.

Reindeer? Really?

I had the opportunity to witness this resistance first-hand with Robert, a close friend of mine. Years ago, I was quite amused to find out that Robert didn't believe in reindeer. To him these beautiful creatures were nothing more than fantastical characters in the story of Santa Clause and, flying or not, they were no more real than the Grinch or the Abominable Snowman.

Forgive me if you happen to be agreeing with Robert here, but reindeer are in fact real. Maybe they don't fly, and you might be hard-pressed to find one with a glowing red nose, but the animals themselves are quite genuine. I remember being taken aback to think that Robert was in denial about such a basic fact, but our beliefs are often based on what we learn growing up, right or wrong, so to me it was just a simple matter of re-educating the man.

A few days later I happened to be walking through downtown Cincinnati. It being the Christmas season, I crossed paths with a Santa walking down the sidewalk with nothing less than a live reindeer. That was all it took, in my mind, at least. At dinner that night I told Robert that I had seen a live reindeer just that afternoon, so, see, they really do exist. Case closed.

I must say, I had certainly under-estimated the depth of the human belief system. Apparently, I was told, it couldn't have been a real reindeer because reindeer don't exist. Maybe, Robert suggested, it was just a deer with antlers tied to its head. (I had visions of Max, the Grinch's dog, in the infamous Dr. Seuss story, with a single awkward antler tied precariously to his head with a piece of string.) "No," I said, "I walked right by it. It was a real reindeer with real antlers growing out of its very real head." I knew what I saw. Maybe, he suggested, it was a small moose or some other creature, but obviously I was mistaken (if not somewhat off my rocker) in thinking that I had seen a reindeer — and of course he had to throw in that I had also seen Santa... Enough said!

I made one final feeble attempt at enlightening this stubborn young man. Looking up reindeer on the Internet, I printed the website page complete with a picture that closely matched the creature I had seen walking with Santa. At least this time I was more prepared when I was, again, shot down. Pictures or not, I was told, reindeer did not exist.

This one disagreement over something as inconsequential as the existence of reindeer left a mark on our relationship;

after all, how could someone who cared about and trusted me not believe that I knew what I had seen? How could he be so closed off to my view of reality, even if it was different than his own? Yes, I think maybe he did question my sanity a bit after that, given that I was so sure I had seen something he knew to be purely the stuff of fiction and children's stories.

I know now that it really wasn't personal, but rather the nature of the human belief system. Simply put, it's not easily altered. Some people are more open to revising their views of reality while others have a much harder time of it. (In this case I think I could have had the world's most renowned zoologist parade a dozen reindeer through his living room and Robert would still have been in denial.) Some people must simply have an experience themselves before they will believe something, but for others even that may not be enough.

To Believe or Not to Believe...

A dichotomy of belief systems such as mine and Robert's can play havoc on a relationship, especially when it comes to more serious subjects like paranormal experiences. Sure, it may be okay if you believe in ghosts and your significant other doesn't. In most cases that doesn't affect our daily lives and we can even relish an occasional good debate on the topic. However, when we experience the paranormal, a dichotomy of beliefs can have a significant impact. Imagine coming to the realization that the house you are living in is haunted and having your spouse or significant other tell you that, like the reindeer, ghosts just don't exist. Your reality and theirs have just collided. The result can often be quite stressful to both parties, but particularly for the one experiencing the paranormal.

To make matters even worse, it's not uncommon for just one person in a household, quite often the woman, to be affected by a haunting while others seem largely unaffected. Suffice it to say, when one person has experiences that are out of the realm of the normal — getting their hair pulled when no one is around, hearing their name called by disembodied voices, or seeing full-bodied apparitions — and no one else in the house is experiencing anything unusual, it is quite common for that person to start questioning their sanity. If your loved ones don't allow for the possibility of the paranormal in their own belief systems, you might easily find yourself feeling very alone.

Before we get too critical of those with beliefs that are different than our own, let's talk a little more about belief systems in general. The experience of finding out something you firmly believed isn't true, such as you were adopted or that your spouse, whom you trusted with all your heart and soul, is untrustworthy, can shake us to our very core and often leads us to questioning our other beliefs. These experiences, which can change our whole lives, are unsettling at best, but in the end they bring us closer to an understanding of reality than we had previously possessed.

Our views on the paranormal can be looked at in much the same way. We learn many of our beliefs from our parents and later from peers and friends, as well as from our own personal experiences (or lack thereof). For anyone raised believing in ghosts, or at least in the possibility of them, one small encounter with the paranormal will likely be quite convincing. However, for those who have had a lifetime of not believing, a sudden shift in their views of reality might be too damaging for them to allow, even after a few paranormal encounters. If, however, these firm non-believers experience something so significant and undeniable that they suddenly truly believe, then that experience will likely be one that changes them forever in many ways.

Over the years I have had many opportunities to talk with those living with the paranormal and I have found one of the most important things I can offer them is simply someone to talk to who doesn't think they're crazy. Most are hesitant at first, testing before they are truly willing to open up. Many start out with phrases such as "This is probably pretty unusual…" or "This is going to sound crazy…" Whatever follows is rarely unusual or crazy.

When I first speak to new clients, I try to put them at ease by letting them know that things similar to what they are experiencing can and do happen to other people, myself included. It is actually not that uncommon and there is a very good chance they are not crazy

after all. This alone can help ease some of the stress.

MOVING INTO A HAUNTED HOUSE

If perchance you discover that you have moved into a haunted house, what should you expect? First, it's very unlikely that you'll find yourself thinking "Ghost!" as soon as you move in. The process of having one family pack up and leave, and a completely different one haul in a house full of boxes and new furnishings, not to mention the new family themselves and any pets they may have brought along, must certainly have some effect on any resident spirit. They might go into hiding, choosing to avoid the havoc all together, or they might jump right on the opportunity to introduce themselves in fun and creative ways, as my New Hope ghost did with its trick with the paint colors. In most cases, though, if anything does seem a bit odd we often simply don't have the time to pay attention to it.

Even at night, when the unpacking and organizing have paused and we're lying quietly in bed, when we hear something odd we aren't likely to jump to the conclusion that our house is haunted. We just don't know what is "normal" there yet, so we can't draw the conclusion of paranormal. Maybe those aren't footsteps — the house might just be settling. The odd scratching sounds might just be a branch rubbing against the side of the house in the breeze. The knocks down the hall might be one of the children, probably unable to sleep well in an unfamiliar room, and the dog's restlessness may simply be because he's overwhelmed with all of the new smells.

Maybe...but then again maybe not. In all honesty, it might not really matter. As long as nothing drastic is happening, the only thing you probably should do is to let things settle down for a few months. In the meantime, you might want to keep a journal or log of anything unusual. Just writing it down and tucking it away may help you let go of it, at least temporarily. Later, when the dust has settled, you can go back over your notes.

You may even want to talk to your family and see what they are experiencing. Of course, you don't want to scare any young children, but it's possible others have been seeing or hearing things also. After that, if you're still worried, it never hurts to do a sage smudging, or a blessing, in any new space you move into, just to clean out any lingering bad energy.

One of the early warning signs worth paying attention to is the behavior of your pets. If they seem to be sensing a presence that you don't, or are exhibiting any of the symptoms discussed earlier, then you may want to consider your own experiences a bit more seriously.

As time passes in your new home, you will begin to get a better feel for the sounds your house makes and what may indeed be symptoms of paranormal activity, but be prepared — not all family members may come to the same conclusion.

SAME HOUSE/DIFFERENT EXPERIENCES

One of the common frustrations I hear from clients is that they seem to be experiencing much more activity than the rest of the family, especially if that client is a woman. Often the woman will be convinced the house is haunted while the man is completely convinced that it's not.

This discrepancy is often due to differing perceptions of the events taking place. One person may feel a cold spot pass by and think it odd while another might think of it as nothing more than a draft. The more you are open to the belief in ghosts and the paranormal, the more likely you are to notice the potential signs. Those who don't believe often offer "logical" explanations for paranormal events even if those explanations make no sense at all.

One theory regarding this unbalance is that women are generally more emotionally sensitive and more likely to possess some level of psychic ability, even if it is latent and they are largely unaware of it. That's not to say a man can't be the focus of the activity or it may not be centered on any one individual at all. It's simply that in a majority of cases I have found the woman of the house is more affected than the man.

Children and teens are the other cases where one individual may experience a disproportionate amount of activity. With children, one theory is that they are more open to the paranormal because they haven't yet been taught, by their parents or by society, that such things don't exist. Another theory is that they are closer to "the other side" because they have more recently come from there and their connections are stronger.

It's also possible that many of these children are gifted and draw or attract spirits. Many people believe that we are all born with some natural psychic abilities that usually go undeveloped and are thus lost. If so, it would make sense that children could be aware of spirit energies that the rest of us can no longer sense. Stories abound of mothers walking into their babies' rooms to find them seemingly playing with someone who isn't there or hearing halves of conversations over the baby monitor. Toddlers sometimes report someone in their room checking on them or reading them a story. Often it is an older adult, likely a crossed-over family member.

Teens are another case altogether. I am convinced that there is something about their physical or emotional energy, or something in how their brains are changing with puberty, that both attracts and energizes earthbound spirits. With a teen or even a pre-teen in the home, it's sometimes as if the resident ghost has been given a shot of B12 or an overdose of caffeine, enabling it to manifest more strongly.

Sometimes when one person begins to experience paranormal activity it's simply because the spirit, for whatever reason, likes them or feels some sort of connection to them. Other times it may just be totally random, having nothing to do with the person at all. They may have just happened to get the one really active room in the house as their bedroom or maybe they do the laundry for the family and thus they spend more time in the basement.

However, in many cases the entire family experiences the haunting, especially if the home is particularly active. It has just always fascinated me how often the experiences are skewed to one or two particular individuals. When that does happen, it makes the situation much more difficult for the family. Anytime you've been through a significant experience and those you love — your own family in fact — doubt you, it can cause significant stress. Understanding that their lack of belief isn't personal may help a bit. Sometimes evidence offered by paranormal investigators can help, too, but there are those who will refuse to believe, no matter what, and you will likely not be able to change their minds.

There is one little trick I have seen work on occasion. Sometimes the person who is the focus of the activity will ask the ghost to do something to convince the other person that it is there — and sometimes it does.

Chapter 6

Calling in the Pros

"… if we can evolve an instrument so delicate as to be affected by our personality as it survives in the next life, such an instrument, when made available, ought to record something."

— *Thomas Edison*

Okay, you have gotten this far and you are still thinking that maybe your house is haunted. You are even considering calling in a paranormal team to investigate. Now what?

Paranormal investigators are generally everyday people with day jobs who spend their nights and weekends helping people like you and hopefully advancing the field of paranormal research while they're at it. We are engineers, business professionals, medical practitioners, musicians, and restaurant workers. Just about anyone you run into might be a paranormal investigator in their spare time. We come from diverse cultural, spiritual, and religious backgrounds; our common thread is a fascination with the paranormal paired with a desire to help people.

Many paranormal investigators became interested in this work because we have had our own personal experiences. Some are trying to make sense out of what happened to them while others realize that their experience was just a small taste of what is possible and seek a greater understanding. Others just have a burning interest in the paranormal accompanied by a desire to have their own experiences. Many of us want to educate people and help remove the many misconceptions out there, and pretty much all of us want to help others who think they may be experiencing paranormal activity or even to help the earthbound spirits themselves.

In the field of paranormal investigation, also known as "ghost hunting," there isn't any formal standardization of what we do or how we do it. In fact, each team is a little different in how they operate. Most groups, however, take their work very seriously and strive to learn from each other. Some teams will only do investigations while others may offer additional support in helping clients deal with their haunting. Some use psychics or mediums while others prefer to stick with only scientific instruments. In general, though, most paranormal investigation teams do three things:

1. *They will ask you questions and talk with you to understand your experiences and concerns, and also answer any questions you might have.*

2. *They come to your home and perform an investigation, usually at night, using all of the equipment and resources at their disposal. In doing so they attempt to both debunk any claims as being due to natural causes and find proof of paranormal activity, should there be any.*

3. *They spend countless hours reviewing the evidence collected and discussing potentially paranormal findings with their team members before returning to share their results with you.*

Additionally, many teams will do research on the history of the location or on anything that may shed light on the case. Many will also offer advice on how to deal with any activity you might be experiencing, perform smudgings (cleansings with sage or incense) or blessings to help lessen the activity, or may help in trying to get the spirit to cross over.

Why do People Call a Paranormal Investigator?

There are many reasons why paranormal teams receive investigation requests. Usually it's a combination of things that have built up over time before someone in the family suggests going for outside help.

One of the most common reasons teams get called is when someone is suffering from the effects of a lack of sleep. As we will see in the Cedar Run case, a ghost can change the way it manifests over time, learning new tricks along the way and tiring of old ones. Sometimes it will be just fine to live with for years, but then it changes up its game and suddenly you're awake half the night. A few weeks or even months of sleepless nights can make almost anyone seek help.

Other reasons people call a paranormal investigation team include:

- *They seek validation, either for themselves (to be sure they aren't crazy) or for their spouses (to prove to them that they aren't crazy).*

- *Their children seem to be experiencing something and they aren't sure if they should be concerned or not.*

- *The activity recently changed or escalated and now is problematic.*

- *They are curious about who is there and why they have stayed.*

- *They had an experience that frightens them or makes them wonder if whatever is in their home might be evil or even demonic.*

- *They just want someone to make it all stop and for the ghost to go away.*

Before making the decision to contact a paranormal investigation team, make sure you understand what you're hoping to get out of the experience. Talk to your family about this — each person may have a different goal. Knowing what you're hoping to achieve will help you in finding the right team and expressing your wishes to the case manager who contacts you.

You should also make sure the whole family is on-board with the investigation process itself before calling. The case manager will probably want to talk to as many people in the family as possible. Of course children are often excluded from this process at the parents' discretion.

Many people are concerned that the investigation itself will stir up the activity. Although that is entirely possible, I have not known it to happen to any significant extent or for more than a day or two, if it was even the investigation that stirred things up in the first place. In fact often it will be a little quieter after the investigation. Perhaps the ghosts realize we're onto them and they're trying to keep a low profile.

Who Do You Call?

Choosing a paranormal investigation team often requires a little homework. You might try asking around. Often a friend or family member might know someone in the field. If so, get the name of the team and check out their website to see what you can learn about them.

More generally people use the Internet to find a team in their area. Try searching "paranormal investigators" or "paranormal researchers" with the name of your state. Many teams focus on specific areas of the state and you can often tell which areas they cover by their name. Other teams are willing to travel further. Here are a few things to keep in mind when looking for a team:

Do they guarantee confidentiality?

Almost every team does, and they should say so on their web page. However, it is up to you to be sure, assuming you don't want your evidence posted on Youtube along with your address and a big photo of your home with the label "HAUNTED!" For the most part, though, paranormal teams take client confidentiality extremely seriously.

What do they charge?

Paranormal investigation teams should not charge for their services. The only exception is if a team asks for compensation for supplies and travel expenses (generally batteries, tolls, and gas). If so, ask for an estimate of these expenses and make sure they aren't traveling a great distance, or be willing to finance the trip if they are. On the flip side, be conscious of the fact that the team members do this as a volunteer service in their spare time.

Is their website professional?

Anyone with a desire to go on a joy ride investigation can put up a website and hope they get a call. Legitimate investigation teams will generally have more elaborate websites, often offering summaries of cases they have investigated and helpful information about hauntings or the investigation process. Be wary of sites with multiple links to paranormal shows and those which prominently offer themselves for paid services or otherwise come across as less then professional.

Do they show their members full names?

It's customary for paranormal investigation teams to list both the first and last names of their investigators. Some of their members may desire more privacy for whatever reason, but at the very least the founders or directors should be listed by first and last name. You have a right to know who's coming into your home.

Get a Number

Most teams won't post their phone contact information on the web site, but if you submit an investigation request and get a phone call, make sure the person on the other end of the line is willing to tell you who they are and give you a number where you can reach them if needed.

WHAT SHOULD YOU EXPECT?

Most paranormal teams begin the process with an investigation request from their website. Some will provide a phone number, but that's much less common. The request will usually ask about your home, your family, and your experiences. It gives the case manager a little background before they call and helps them organize the questions they want to ask ahead of time.

In the initial conversation, the case manager will want to learn more about what the family is experiencing. They may also be evaluating what you've told them to judge the likelihood of paranormal activity. It's a good time for you to ask

Mike Pabian checks the EMF levels in a bedroom with reported paranormal activity.

questions — about ghosts in general, about your situation, and about the team and how they operate. Make sure you're comfortable with their responses. If not, find another team.

If the team decides to move forward with your case, they often begin with a preliminary visit to your home, also known as a "Prelim." Usually this will involve a visit from one or two representatives from the team who will talk to the family, take a tour of the location, check EMF levels, and possibly even record a little to see if they happen to catch anything.

This initial home visit will allow the team to determine the optimum number of people to bring on the investigation, understand how sound flows through the house, and start planning equipment placement. It will also help them associate the experiences you've shared with the location where they happened. Often they will begin the process of looking for natural causes of any unexplained events.

Following the Prelim, the team will usually schedule the investigation itself. Generally investigations are done on Friday or Saturday nights, driven, if nothing else, by the fact that most investigators have day jobs. There is usually flexibility, though, if there are other needs or considerations. My team generally targets starting at 8 p.m. and wrapping up not long after midnight, with case-by-case flexibility as needed.

Clients often wonder if that time-frame will result in any evidence if most of their activity is in the early morning hours, as is common. Most teams find that even while investigating during the late evening hours, they will still find evidence of paranormal activity. In special cases, of course, most teams will make exceptions. Each case is different and the investigation should be driven by the needs of the client and the particulars of the case.

During the investigation the team leader will usually want the family to remain in one part of the house and refrain from watching television (unless headphones are used) or engaging in any activity that would cause a lot of movement or noise. Pets may also need to be somewhat contained. If the team hears or sees something unusual when reviewing the evidence, but the family was moving around the house or otherwise making noise, the evidence must be discarded as inconclusive. The only way the investigators can be sure what they find has no natural cause is in a controlled environment. Often clients will keep themselves occupied by reading or will use headphones as they listen to music, watch TV, or work on the computer.

When the investigation is over, the team packs up and says their goodbyes. Often they will tell you little or nothing about any experiences they have had that evening. For one thing, they don't want to leave you scared should anything interesting have happened. For another, many prefer to review all of the evidence and consider it as a whole before sharing anything.

Once the team leaves the waiting begins. Evidence review is usually done in the team members' spare time, and thus will likely take several weeks. Each investigator on the case is likely to need anywhere from eight to forty hours to review their own evidence, depending on how much equipment they used. They will also spend considerable time reviewing the evidence their teammates find. The results will then need to be evaluated as a whole and compiled for presentation to the client, at a meeting referred to as the "Reveal."

Most teams will ask that you grant them permission to post a summary of your case, along with their findings, on their website. This should be done in a way to protect your identity, with teams often referring to the case by the name of the town and excluding any details that would reveal the client's name or address. If you're uncomfortable with this, let the case manger know up front. If they will not take your case otherwise, find another team. Most people are perfectly comfortable with it, though, and it's a great way to share results with friends and family.

It's important to note that if a team doesn't find anything during an investigation it doesn't necessarily mean you don't have paranormal activity. It's possible that whatever was there made a significant effort not to be discovered on that particular evening or maybe the circumstances weren't right, for some reason we don't understand. It does happen that an initial investigation yields nothing while a later investigation is quite fruitful. Most teams are willing to come back at a later date if the activity continues.

THE EVIDENCE

The goal of any investigation is twofold: To debunk any claims, when possible, and to collect evidence of paranormal activity, should there be any. Let's touch briefly on what paranormal investigators mean when they talk about "evidence."

The standard for "evidence" varies from team to team. In the paranormal field, we usually call anything that we cannot otherwise explain "evidence." An orb in a photo may or may not be paranormal, but we can usually offer that it may just be dust. Thus it may be interesting if a disproportionate number of photos show orbs, but it is generally not considered to be evidence of anything paranormal.

At the other extreme, if a recording includes the clear voice of someone not present at the time, then that's likely to be considered as evidence of the paranormal. Alone it may not be enough to conclude that there is indeed a ghost in your house, but it's generally considered to be indicative of something unusual going on. After all, voices from nowhere are certainly not normal.

In ghost hunting, we consider each unexplainable photo, video anomaly, or audio clip to be potential evidence. We then evaluate the collection of evidence as a whole before determining if we believe there is paranormal activity at a location. Let's consider unexplained knocking as an example. If we hear a knock coming from the attic, we might investigate. Assuming we can't find a cause, we may consider that interesting, but it's certainly not proof of anything paranormal. It could have been the house settling, an acorn falling on the roof, or just about anything else. However, what if we are doing an EVP session and we hear a loud knock-knock-knock from the adjoining room, even though no one is in that area of the home? We again investigate and find nothing amiss. This might be a little more convincing, but it's still far from proof of anything.

Now assume we sit down in the room that we just heard the knock coming from and we ask whomever might be there to knock twice to let us know they are there. If we get two knocks as a response, and if we can find no logical explanation, most ghost hunters would be willing to present that to their clients as potential evidence. Still, if that's the only thing that happens that night, they might be hard-pressed to declare that the location has paranormal activity.

What if they ask multiple questions and more often than not they get a knock in response? What if they ask questions such as "How many pennies are on the floor in front of me?" to eliminate the possibility that some trickster is listening in and knocking just to be having a little fun? If they get the right number of knocks, then many people would be significantly more convinced and, when that particular experience is viewed with other pieces of evidence including unexplained lights or EVPs, then a verdict of "paranormal activity" might certainly be warranted.

Let's review some of the more common types of evidence that paranormal investigators look for.

Ghosts on Film

Sometimes apparitions, for whatever reason, cannot be seen by the visible eye, but are still picked up on film. This is conceptually similar to EVPs, those voices or sounds not heard by the human ear at the time but which are nonetheless captured on recording devices.

Ghostly apparitions caught on film are among the most controversial types of paranormal evidence. It's rare to capture a full-bodied apparition or shadow person, but why shouldn't it be? Actual sightings are also rare. Other types of possible photographic evidence include mists, shadows, dark clouds, unexplained lights, orbs, and shapes of faces.

This light anomaly captured at Top O' The World in Bath, Ohio, is unusual in its path and colors. *Photo courtesy of Bea Brugge and World Paranormal Investigations.*

Human-shaped figures are probably the most convincing photographic evidence, especially if captured in a controlled environment such as a paranormal investigation. They are also easily faked. Mists are often seen in photos taken outdoors and more often than not can be attributed to natural causes such as water vapor in the air or even simply the breath of the photographer.

Shadows and dark clouds can be interesting and fun to try and debunk. It's difficult to draw any conclusion about whether they are paranormal or not unless you are familiar with the circumstances under which they were taken. Paranormal investigators habitually snap two or three photos in a row so that if an anomaly does appear in one, the others will provide a baseline for comparison.

Orbs are one of the most debated types of photographic evidence of the paranormal. The vast majority of orbs in photos are not paranormal at all, but rather caused by the reflection of the flash or another light source off of dust, water droplets, small insects or even pollen. As a result, whether an orb is paranormal or perfectly natural in source is often impossible to tell.

Orbs are often caused by dust particles that are physically close to both the camera lens and light source, generally within a few feet. If you see an orb in a photograph and it's further back from the camera, as can be evidenced because it is partially hidden behind a solid object, then it isn't a dust or particle reflection.

The way in which our photographic equipment interprets paranormal energy can have many other variations as well. This exterior photo was taken by Bea Brugge, cofounder and director of World Paranormal Investigations, while on a ghost hunt at Top O' The World, a notoriously haunted site in Bath, Ohio. The light streaks are brightly colored, the wider ones being an almost aqua blue color while the narrow streaks are a bright lime green. Whatever energy caused this result was moving at a very high speed, as is often the case with energies thought to be paranormal.

Some light anomalies can be seen with the naked eye and are also referred to as orbs. The size can vary from a pinpoint of bright light to that of a grapefruit or even a soccer ball. They tend to move quickly and disappear just as quickly. As much as orbs in photographs are often quite unconvincing, orbs caught on video can sometimes be quite intriguing. Sometimes we'll capture an odd small light moving across the frame in a pattern uncharacteristic of dust or bugs. While that shouldn't ever be evidence enough to conclude a house to be haunted, it is certainly worth consideration, especially if it is coincident with other activity.

EVPs

Actually seeing ghosts is always fun, but hearing them is somehow much more likely, so let's talk a little about EVPs. In 1920, Thomas Edison, inventor of the electric light, the phonograph, and the motion picture camera, was working on a machine to achieve spirit communication with the dead. In an interview in the October 1920 issue of *The American Magazine*, Edison shared, "I have been at work for some time building an apparatus to see if it is possible for personalities which have left this earth to communicate with us."

Edison was definitely onto something. Today digital recorders are the mainstay of most paranormal investigators' toolkits with EVPs continuing to fascinate even the most experienced ghost hunters. If you have watched any of the ghost hunting shows, you are sure to be familiar with the concept. In locations thought to be haunted a device such as a digital voice recorder is used during the investigation. On playback, sounds and voices not originally heard by the investigators are somehow audible. Some are mere murmurs or whispers and what is being said is anybody's guess, but others are as loud and clear as those of the living.

Although I'm convinced that some EVPs are indeed either earthbound or crossed-over spirits — both seem equally capable of leaving their auditory imprint — I agree with many others in the field who would argue that we simply don't know the true source of much of what we capture.

For example, some EVPs can be residual in nature. In the Woodbury case we'll be reviewing in Chapter 9, I recorded our conversations as we sat at the dining room table discussing the family's experiences. Although no music was playing at the time, on the recording the sound of a waltz fades in, plays for a few moments, and then fades back out again. Music is certainly not the voice of the dead; the true source of the sound can be theorized, but is, so far, unknown.

There are, of course, other possibilities that might explain the intriguing phenomena of EVPs. Perhaps these are the voices of angels...or perhaps demons. Maybe they are voices from an entirely different time or place that just happened to leak through a rift in the fabric of time or space. Or maybe they're some sort of extraterrestrial communication, or even our own thoughts somehow embedded on the recording device. All we can say, when it comes right down to it, is that as fascinating as EVPs may be we simply don't know the source of their creation.

EMF Spikes

Another thing ghost hunters look for is spikes in the baseline EMF levels. There are several tools that perform this function, most commonly an EMF meter, a K-II Meter, and a Trifield Meter. The Trifield Meters display the exact EMF level while the K-II meters use colored lights to indicate general EMF level ranges. The theory is that ghosts are energy and sometimes these meters will pick up the presence of unexplainable energy as indicated by

The multi-colored lights on a K-II Meter allow investigators to monitor EMF levels in a dark room. It can also be used in spirit communication.

increased EMF levels. Investigators will often try to use EMF spikes to open spirit communication. They ask questions that the ghost can answer by getting close to the device and making the levels spike.

The Flashlight Game

A fun game that ghost hunters play involves using a flashlight as a communication tool. To successfully do this, the flashlight needs to be the kind that turns on and off with a twist of the end, such as a Maglite®. Adjust the flashlight so that it's on the verge of being turned on and set it on the floor or another stable surface free from vibrations and then attempt to get any spirits that might be around to turn the flashlight on and off.

The drawback here is that any little vibration might possibly have the same effect. To be sure any potential activity is indeed paranormal, investigators usually require the responses to be repeated and consistent. If two flashlights are placed on different surfaces and both are turned on or off on command, the activity is much more convincing.

Other Fun Stuff

Ghost hunters have become quite adept at creating and adapting equipment especially for their needs. Digital thermometers are used to detect and measure temperature changes. Geophones sense vibrations such as footsteps. Laser grids can be projected in front of video cameras to better see any disturbances that pass in front of them. A "Ghost Box" or "Frank's Box" is a radio modified to continually scan through stations and is used as a sound and word base on which spirit voices can sometimes be heard. Pendulums and divining or dowsing rods, simple mechanical devices that have been around for centuries, are still used by some paranormal investigators today. However, more and more new "toys" are invented each year.

DOING YOUR OWN INVESTIGATION

If you're hesitant about having strangers in your home or have any other concerns about bringing in a paranormal investigation team, you may want to do a little investigating on your own. A word of caution, though: Investigating your own home is, in effect, encouraging communication between the spirits and the residents and may subsequently increase the activity at the location. Many paranormal investigators choose not to participate in investigations of their own houses just for this reason. Others, such as myself, are more comfortable with the concept. Over the years I have done several mini-investigations of my home with family, friends, and fellow investigators with no ill effects, but every location is different. If you decide to give it a try, set aside an evening to investigate and then stop. If the activity hasn't increased and you want to try it again, wait a month or two, but also limit your investigation attempts. Investigating is a means of communication and continued efforts could amplify the activity.

You may want to begin by keeping a log or diary of any paranormal activity. Have everyone start keeping track of anything they experience and compare notes. This may not only give you a better understanding of what's happening, but you will also identify any hot spots, which will be places you will want to investigate.

In the meantime, begin doing a little research. Talk to neighbors, former

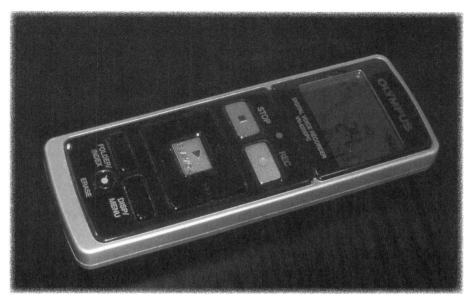
A digital recorder is a staple in a paranormal investigator's toolbox.

residents, even friends and family you've had over, especially if they've stayed overnight. There may be something they've experienced that they just weren't sure they should mention. Next, research the historical records of the house and property. If you live in the United States, you'll want to start with your county courthouse. Before you make the trip you might want to see if any of your county's records are available online.

It's usually best to start with land records. You'll need your property ID number (check your tax bill). Take this to the Register of Deeds department and you should be able to find historical deed and mortgage information for your property. Note the names of each of the owners along with any relevant dates as far back as you can go. Next take these names and go to the Department of Vital Statistics or its equivalent. Try to find the Death Certificate for each individual to see where the death occurred, as well as how and when they passed. Anyone who died while living on the property is obviously of interest. Learn as much as you can about them.

You can now use this information during your investigation. If any former owners or other occupants died in the home, you can address them by name to see if you get a response. You can also use the names of the state and town they were originally born in, or the names of any spouses or children, in an attempt to connect to the spirit on an emotional level.

When you are ready for the actual investigation, you will need an audio recording device. You're best bet is to buy or borrow a digital recorder, preferably one with a USB uplink capability. If that's not possible, most smart phones have recording capabilities. For a few bucks' investment, you can buy an app that offers even more functionality for recording and playback. If you have none of these, an analog tape recorder may be a little more cumbersome, but will work just as well.

If you have a K-II Meter or EMF detector, you'll also want to use that.

If not, you might want to pick up a compass and a small LED flashlight. Have someone shine the flashlight on the compass during the investigation. This will allow you to see any movement of the needle in the dark without shedding too much light or ruining anyone's night vision. Small finger lights also work well for this and are fairly inexpensive.

If you have a flashlight that turns on and off by twisting the end, you might want to use that as a communication tool as well. Also, you will want a flashlight to have handy as a light source.

Now do a little planning. Pick one or two areas of your home that are most active. Plan ahead for when you would like to do the investigation. Make sure everyone will be participating or will cooperate by remaining completely quiet or being somewhere far from the investigation area. If you have pets, see if someone will take them for the evening or try to find a place to keep them contained and quiet.

On the night of the investigation, set everything up in your first location and turn out as many lights as you're comfortable with. It's usually easiest to have everyone sit facing the center of the room with the equipment — your recorder, EMF detector, and flashlight — in the middle of a table or on the floor. Begin recording and clearly state the date, time, location, and the names of the people in the room. Make sure the recorder is stationary and is not being held by anyone.

As soon as you have started recording, you will also need to start "tagging" every noise by simply noting it on the recording. It's usually best if one person is given the responsibility for general noises while everyone also tags any noises they make personally. If someone's stomach grumbles, tag it. If a car passes by, a dog barks, the house creaks... tag, tag, tag.

One additional rule during an EVP session is that there is absolutely no whispering. This will probably be difficult at first. It's dark and quiet and you're listening for any unusual sounds, so using a whispered voice may seem quite natural, but speak in a normal tone at your usual volume. Whispers sound really freaky on playback and are often mistaken for EVPs. If you accidentally whisper, tag it.

Now adjust the flashlight so it is in the off position, but will turn on with the slightest twist; assign someone the job of tagging any flashlight activity. You might even make up a system of tags, such as "full on" if the light comes all the way on all at once, "half on" for when it's slowly coming on but isn't quite there yet (sometimes it takes a while), and "dimming" and "full off" for the opposite effects.

Similarly, have someone assigned to watch the EMF meter and tag any movement of the needle (or lights on the K-II meter). If you are able to film the session, make sure the flashlight and K-II meter are in view and you can omit all of that tagging — you will just want some record of any activity.

When everyone is settled, begin the EVP session. Start by announcing that you're speaking to whomever is in the room with you. Introduce yourselves and explain that you do not intend to do them any harm, but would simply like to communicate and learn who they are and why they are there. Let them know that the equipment you have will not hurt them, but that it can help confirm their presence.

Tell them that the flashlight is something that is there for them to play with and that if they can learn to turn it on and off you can communicate with them that way. Also let them know that if they speak or shout into the recorder, you might be able to hear them later when you listen to the recording.

Now begin asking questions. Go slowly, leaving ten or fifteen seconds between each query. It may seem like a long time, but responses are not always immediate. Start with basic questions such as "What is your name?" and "How old are you?" If you have the names of anyone who may have died in the house or any information about previous owners, use that in your questioning.

Sometimes questions that have more emotional impact will get a response when others don't. Try "Do you miss your family?" or "Are you lonely?" and other questions along those lines. You might also ask what year it is, what year were they born, or who the President is in hopes of determining when they lived. Ask about their death; ask if they know they are dead or about how they died. Finally, ask them if they need help or if they have a message for anyone.

When you have completed a series of questions, also known as an EVP session, change things up a bit and ask them if they can turn on the flashlight. If the light does turn on then, or at any time during the night, be sure to say "thank you" and ask them to turn it back off as verification. If you can get them to turn the flashlight on and off on demand, you can move on to other questions requiring yes and no responses. Keep in mind that the light may also be turning on due to vibrations in the floor, so you need to have some consistent interaction before you can consider the activity to be potentially paranormal.

You might also ask the spirit to knock for you. If you do and you hear a knock, ask it to knock again. If the knock is repeated, explain that you'd like to ask it a few questions and that one knock will mean an answer of "yes" while two knocks will mean "no." If you are lucky enough to get a communication session started this way, ask a few questions

and then repeat some of your previous questions. If you get different answers different times, the knocking may not be paranormal at all, or whoever it is may simply be messing with you. In any case, you'll need to be a little less trusting of the answers you may be receiving if the responses aren't consistent.

Always be polite and say "please" and "thank you" during an investigation. (Once after saying "thank you" I even got an EVP that said "welcome.") Also, never *ever* provoke… Provoking is trying to elicit a spirit's response with taunts or negative comments such as "You're a coward!" or "I wouldn't be surprised if you committed suicide." If you have watched paranormal TV shows, some of them tend to do a good measure of provoking and it often gets a response. However, it is also likely to leave the place a bit more stirred up than before the investigation, so never provoke in someone else's home or place of business. You should certainly never do it in your own home, and if you invite a paranormal investigation team in and find them doing it, I would encourage you to escort them right out the door. You are the one who needs to live there after the team has gone.

Whatever you do, please don't include an Ouija Board in your investigation or attempt any sort of a séance unless the session is being conducted by someone experienced in such communications. No paranormal investigation team wants to get called in because someone was doing their own investigation and opened a portal, making the activity worse.

During the investigation, if you are comfortable with it, you may ask the spirit to touch you. Please don't even ask, though, if actually getting touched is going to scare the bejeebies out of you or anyone else in the room. Also never invite spirits to touch someone else in the group — that's their prerogative, not yours — and never offer to let them use your energy. That could start you down a dangerous path, especially with a spirit you need to live with.

When you complete the investigation in the first location, take a break before continuing, or stop there and wrap it up for the night. When you are finished, stop your audio recorder and either upload the file or e-mail it to yourself, depending on the device your using, so you don't accidentally delete it. If possible, save the original on the device as a backup.

When you are ready to do the evidence review, you will want to use headphones or at least ear buds. These are considered essential equipment. You might certainly hear an EVP without the headphones, but the added clarity will make the entire process easier and you're more likely to notice softer voices that might otherwise have been missed. Some EVPs can be amazingly clear, but very, very quiet.

Audio evidence review can be done by playing the recording back directly from the device it was recorded on or from a computer if the file has been uploaded. However, for best results, you'll want something a little more professional. Consider downloading the free or trial version of either "Audacity" or "WavePad." You should be able to find either with a quick search engine query.

To learn the basics of how to use this software for EVPs, try YouTube — there are several videos out there that make getting started fairly easy. These programs will display the wave patterns of the recording and will allow you to more easily stop, pause, or jump to a specific location. If you do find something of interest, you can copy just that portion of the recording into its own file to save to share with others. If you want to get fancy, you can slow a recording down, amplify it, or use built-in noise reduction functionality.

Listening for EVPs is a bit of an art in itself. If this is your first time, you may want to listen to the entire recording twice. Listen for words or phrases that were not part of the conversation at the time, especially if the voice sounds odd or distorted or doesn't belong to anyone who was present during the investigation. You might hear whispering that sounds like a conversation but isn't quite audible, voices talking over a conversation, or answers to questions you asked. Also listen for bangs or other odd sounds that weren't heard at the time.

If you do find something you think is unusual, play it for someone else who was there. They may better remember that someone had said that very thing or might know the source of the odd noise.

If your investigation is fruitful and you get EVPs or other activity, this may help verify that something is indeed sharing your home with you. Instead of letting that scare you, try seeing what your evidence helped you learn about whoever is there.

Did you hear the voice of only one spirit or were there more? Was it male or female? Younger or older? Did they offer any clues as to who they were or why they are here?

Even if your house is haunted, you would be lucky to get more than a few EVPs in a single session such as this. If you don't get any, though, remember that doesn't mean there's nothing there. Whoever it is might have simply chosen not to interact with you or wasn't able to.

One of the benefits of calling in the pros is that they usually come with quite a bit of equipment. They can cover much larger areas with audio surveillance and set up video in the hot spots. They'll probably have some other specialized equipment as well and will be more experienced at controlling the environment, tagging, and evidence analysis.

Mike Pabian, me, and Jennifer Purcell take some time after our investigation of the Groveville home, which is discussed in Chapter 11.

Chapter Seven

What Should You Do if Your House is Haunted?

"Everything that the modern mind cannot define it regards as insane."

— *Carl Jung*

Maybe you are one hundred percent certain that your house is haunted or maybe you are just starting to get nudged in that direction. Perhaps you simply don't care if it's some strange ghost or your great grandmother bumping and thumping all night long — you just want it to stop.

Dealing with spirits can be a bit tricky, but it's not too different than dealing with the living. It is just sometimes harder to understand who you are dealing with and what they want, especially with communication being a huge issue.

When it comes to the paranormal, there are no one-size-fits-all solutions. However, it helps to understand as much as you can about the energies in your home. The historical research and investigation techniques discussed in the previous chapter can often help in that respect, but even if you don't have any information about your resident spirit there are still some things you can try. One word of caution, though. If you have any reason to believe you might be dealing with something demonic, please consult a specialist before trying anything on your own. These are completely different entities than the earthbound spirits this chapter is addressing and need to be handled as such. Also be forewarned that although these strategies are usually helpful in mitigating unwanted activity, they do have the potential to backfire and make things worse.

Laying Down the Law

The first thing I usually recommend is simply talking to your ghost. Even if you're not sure if there is one, act as if you are. Begin by taking ownership of the space and laying down the law. I'm not saying to tell them that it's your house now and they need to leave. Unfortunately it's their

house, too. If they do comply, you may have just kicked out a small child or an elderly woman. If they don't cooperate, you have just set a very negative tone to the relationship.

Earthbound spirits were people once, too. We really don't know why they're here, but they are and compassion goes a lot further than dominance in most cases. Of course if you have reason to believe your ghost is a recent addition that followed you home from somewhere, then feel free to tell it that it doesn't belong there and to go back to wherever it came from. However, if it was there first, it might be best to try a different approach.

Start by laying some ground rules. First, identify the one or two issues you most want to get under control. If there are children in your home make this your first priority. If you're especially bothered by overnight visits, include this as well.

Begin any conversation by acknowledging their existence. That way they know they've been heard and may stop trying so hard to get your attention. Then address them directly, with a firm but compassionate tone in a normal speaking volume (refrain from addressing them with anger or extreme emotion). It's not too different than addressing a toddler and setting house rules.

Let's say your spirit friend wakes you up in the middle of the night by knocking and banging all around the house. Try saying something like this:

"I need to speak to the spirit sharing my home. I know you are here, but this is my house now. I am willing to try and share it with you, but only if you follow some basic rules. I need my sleep at night and you're keeping me awake. Once I go to bed you

need to be perfectly quiet and leave me alone. If you want to get my attention, you can knock on the walls in the morning once everyone is awake, but at night you must not disturb us."

Some of you may be shuddering at the part about offering to let them knock away in the morning. If that bothers you, just leave that part out or tell them they can knock once or twice. However you might have more success by offering them an alternative outlet for their energy. If you catch your new puppy chewing on a shoe, you scold her and replace it with a doggie bone because, after all, puppies need to chew. Well, some ghosts need to interact. Concentrate on getting the situation under control and getting some sleep first before taking your efforts to the next level.

Often a good laying down of the law is all it takes. Add your speech to your bedtime ritual each night. Try it for a few days, even a week. If you still haven't had positive results, you can start being a little stronger in your delivery of the message, but please don't resort to yelling and screaming — it may backfire. However, if you are experiencing anything that is either frightening or threatening, I would recommend calling a professional or at least blessing the house or performing a smudging.

SMUDGING AND INCENSE

Smudging shares its roots with the burning of incense; both traditions date back thousands of years. Smudging is a powerful Native American cleansing and purifying technique that uses a bundle of dried herbs called a smudge stick. Sage is most commonly used, but cedar,

juniper, lavender, and sweet grass are also popular, as is a blending of two or more of these.

Incense is commonly used today in many organized religions. Christian churches use the rising smoke as a symbol of the prayer of the faithful rising to heaven. In Asia, incense is used in religious settings to purify the surroundings. Hindus also use it in prayer and worship. Smudging and incense are far from "New Age" type cleansing rituals.

There are many variations on how to perform a smudging, but the basic concept of each is to fill every part of your home with the smoke from the smoldering smudge stick. You could also smudge just one or two rooms for lighter needs.

To perform a smudging start with a heavy ceramic dish or bowl to catch the smoldering sage. Make sure the dish will not become overly hot and the ashes and embers will be contained. A light base of sand can be useful for these purposes. Light the end of the smudge stick and let it catch, then extinguish any flames and let it smolder much like incense. Be cautious of any embers. If the smoke ceases at any time during the smudging, simply relight it.

Holding the smudge stick firmly, start in the uppermost area of your house, usually the attic. Open a window in each room, if possible, to let the smoke carry out any negative energy. Circle the room — some prefer a clockwise direction — using your hand or a large feather to push the smoke throughout the room. Be extremely mindful of any lit embers or ashes that may fly off. If your home burns down, you'll have lost everything, but the ghost will likely still be hanging around.

As you move around the room, push the smoke high and low, taking extra care to get it into the corners. Open closets and cabinets and push the

A smudge stick, such as the one shown here, can often quell any paranormal activity in a home, although the smudging process might need to be repeated over time.

smoke in there also. Move down through the floors of your home ending up at the front door and opening it to whisk away the smoke as you finish. If you have a basement, do this last, working your way up towards the front door. When you've finished be sure to extinguish the smudge stick completely.

Incense can be used in much the same way as a smudge stick, some say with equal effectiveness. Choose Lavender, Sandalwood or Sage cones (sticks are fine, but are just a little more difficult to use). Place the incense in a small bowl or dish, or use a censure. A tea ball can serve as a makeshift censure if the bottom is lined with tin foil.

In extremely active environments, my preference is to sage the entire home first, then to burn incense in the bedrooms or other active areas daily or just before bed until things are under control.

THE WHITE LIGHT OF PROTECTION

This is one of the most powerful techniques for fending off negative or unwanted energy. It may take a little effort and repetition to master, but even your initial attempts can be quite effective. If you think you may be at all sensitive or intuitive, you may want to look into additional energy and grounding techniques as well.

The white light of protection uses your own personal energy, supplemented with the energy of God or the Creator, to surround you with a protective shell of positive energy. Once mastered, this technique can also be used to protect your family, your home, and anyone you choose. There are many variations of this exercise. Feel free to use this one as is or modified to your liking. They are equally as effective in their result if the energy and intent is there.

> *Begin by visualizing a bright light in the very core of your body. Feel it fed from your own energy or from that of God or the Creator in whom you believe. The source of your energy is limitless and pure. Imagine it growing stronger and brighter.*
>
> *Now extend the light to cocoon your body. Feel its strength, warmth, and brightness as you push it out and surround yourself with its purity and protection. Hold the energy there for a few minutes before releasing it. As you do so it will remain, surrounding you with a protective shield.*

Practice this once or twice a day and the energy you produce will become stronger. If you're bothered by spirits during the night, do this before going to sleep. As you get stronger with your energy push the light surrounding your body out further and further until it fills your entire room. You can do this for your children's rooms as well. At first, you might want to do it while physically present, but as you gain strength you should be able to do it from wherever you are.

Your own energy is strong and is sourced from a place more powerful than we can imagine. Use your own spiritual and religious beliefs to draw from this source. Any earthbound spirits in your home are simply energy themselves and this technique can produce amazing results in establishing barriers.

PRAYERS

No matter what your religious or spiritual beliefs may be, prayer is extremely powerful. Even if everyone in the household believes something different, if they are all connecting to the higher power through prayer, meditation, or any other means, then the results can be amazing.

In some cases prayer alone may be all you need to deal with an entity, especially a negative one. A house blessing can go a long way or may halt things entirely. In the case of earthbound spirits, though, sometimes it takes a little more. That's not to disrespect the power of prayer, but these spirits are just disembodied souls not yet crossed-over. You can pray for them just as you would pray for anyone else, but should they choose not to go into the light, prayers may not stop them from stomping around or slamming doors at night.

Prayers are a very personal choice. Here are two of my favorites, but you should use whatever you are comfortable with.

> ## Unity Prayer for Protection
> ### (James Dillet Freeman)
>
> *The light of God surrounds me;*
> *The love of God enfolds me;*
> *The power of God protects me;*
> *The presence of God watches*
> *   over me;*
> *Wherever I am, God is!*

Blessings and Holy Water

Having a clergyman perform a house blessing is never a bad idea, but doing your own blessing can sometimes serve you just as well in quelling a restless spirit. Such a blessing is simply one way of taking authority over your home, and in this case you're dedicating your home to the Lord and asking his Spirit to fill your home, pushing out anything negative or evil.

The blessing can be done with or without Holy Water. To obtain Holy Water you'll want to visit your nearest Catholic Church, bringing a small bottle from home. Being quiet and respectful of the environment, locate the large container of Holy Water which will be in a public area. Fill your container and leave a donation of a dollar or two if you possibly can.

Some people prefer to combine a house blessing with a smudging. Alternatively, incense can be placed in a censure and swung lightly to distribute the smoke. If you choose this method, follow the same basic routine as with the smudging, offering a prayer of your choice in each room, and, if desired, sprinkling the holy water or dipping a finger in it and making the sign of the cross over each door and window as you move through your home.

BELLS

Another method of breaking up the negative energy in a home is with the use of bells. As with incense, bells are also used in many religious rituals. Ringing a bell in an enclosed area can help break up and dissipate negative energy. Any bell will do, but many, myself included, prefer tingsha cymbals, which have been used for centuries in Tibetan Buddhism for prayer and meditation. These small cymbals are typically 2-1/2 to 4 inches in diameter and are attached together with a leather cord. When the edges are struck together as the cymbals are held perpendicular to each other they produce a clear high pitched tone perfect for transforming an environment.

For those adverse to the scent of sage or incense, the ringing of bells in each corner of a room to clear a space can be a good alternative. I prefer to use both, breaking up the negative energy in a room with the tingshas just before smudging.

Tingsha cymbals produce a long pure sound that is believed to break-up negative energy.

Clutter be Gone!

If you're the kind of person who keeps a clean and organized house day in and day out, good for you! You can skip this section. For the rest of us, though, one place to start might be with a little cleaning and decluttering. No, you're not trying to make the place a little homier for your uninvited guest. Spirits are energy and, if we have one around, we need to increase the positive energy in the home and eliminate any negative energy as much as possible.

There are two primary reasons for decluttering. First, dust-filled nooks and crannies, piles of unsorted paperwork, boxes stacked in corners, and surfaces overflowing with clutter can all create places for negative energy to gather. A little negative energy here and there may be okay, but sometimes it gets to the point where there's just too much and the small pockets of negativity seem to meld into a cloud of the nasty stuff creating a heaviness in the room.

Secondly, think of how you feel when you walk into a dirty, disheveled room. It's not a good feeling, is it? Its heaviness is a burden, weighing you down. You may even notice your shoulders hunching forward and your head hanging slightly as you enter. The negative environment affects your mood and your energy, and your mood and energy in turn affect the environment.

Now imagine walking into that same room when it's clean and clutter free. You almost can't help but envision yourself taking a deep breath, shoulders back, head held higher. The air feels lighter and fresher. Now you're radiating that positive energy back into the environment.

The idea of suddenly transforming your home into a clean and clutter-free oasis of tranquility may be a bit overwhelming, especially if you are already sleep deprived from any ghostly nighttime antics, so start small and pick one room. If the children are complaining of being awoken at night, by all means begin with their bedrooms. If you see, hear, or feel unseen energies in your own bedroom, that may be a good place to start. Otherwise choose the room that the family spends the most time in, often either the family room or the kitchen. Concentrate on clearing and cleaning that one space and you might be surprised how much that helps. When you're finished, enjoy the results and then move onto the next room when you can.

Call a Truce

Every family has their differences and their squabbles. In fact, simply having a ghost around can sometimes escalate the quarreling, since there might be added tension because of the different viewpoints of family members regarding the activity. It could also be due to the added stress that multiple sleepless nights quickly brings on.

Talk to your spouse, significant other, or your family about it, but be sure to approach it in neutral terms. Something along the lines of "I realize things have been tense around here lately and we've all been on each other's cases a lot." (If you start with a sentence that implies the blame is on the other party and you own no part of it, you're finished before you've started.)

Ask for a truce for a few days, even a week, with each person being willing to let their differences go, at least temporarily. Start by making a concerted effort yourself, even if no one else seems to be following your lead. Quarreling and fighting build up negativity much as do dust and clutter. The more negativity you can remove from the environment, the more successful you'll be in calming any unwanted activity.

SALT AND SALT SPRAYS

Salt has long been thought to ward off ghosts. Its crystalline structure may certainly have something to do with it, but whatever the reason, many people swear by it. A line of salt around the exterior of your home or across your thresholds is said to keep ghosts out. Of course if you already have such company it will have the opposite effect. A little salt sprinkled around the bedroom, however, might help you get a better night's sleep.

Saltwater is often used for warding off ghosts as well. Dissolve a quarter teaspoon of salt in a pint of water and spray it around the room. If you live in an apartment spray the walls, ceilings and floors between yourself and your neighbors if you feel spirits might be coming through. I prefer sea salt, but even regular table salt will do, and a little saltwater goes a long way. Do be cautious around delicate fabrics and surfaces, though.

NEW EXPECTATIONS

One trick I sometimes recommend for living with ghosts, and have used myself, is to change one's expectations. Most people expect, for example, that when everyone in the family is in bed no one should be banging around the house making noise. So change that. Decide to accept the possibility that someone else is around twenty-four/seven and that they occasionally make too much noise at night. Then take it to the next level — give them a name and an identity.

Maybe call them 'Uncle Frank.' Picture a skinny old gentleman in a bathrobe and slippers, hard of hearing, not quite all there upstairs anymore, who has come to live with you. When you go to bed at night, expect that Uncle Frank is still up — he's a bit of an insomniac — and expect that he's forgetful about letting others have their rest. Sometimes he turns on the TV, slams the kitchen cabinets, or shuffles around too loudly. Who knows, you may actually not be far off. Although unexpected bumps in the night can be frightening, expected bumps are just annoying.

If Uncle Frank is still a little intimidating, then maybe a quiet little silver-haired woman might be more to your taste. Let's call her Grandma Tucker, a sweet older woman who watches over the family now that her own children are grown and gone. If you walk into a room to find the furniture rearranged, well there goes Grandma Tucker again redecorating to her own liking. As for all that banging on the walls? Well she can be annoying rapping that cane of hers around like nobody's business, can't she?

When we expect that ghosts aren't real, or that they are scary or evil, we interpret their activity much differently than we do if we simply accept them for what they are — souls not yet ready to cross over into the next world that have chosen your home as their own.

Chapter Eight

Spirit Rescue

"Life is pleasant. Death is peaceful. It's the transition that's troublesome."

— *Isaac Asimov*

The field of "Spirit Rescue" — helping earthbound spirits crossover to the other side — is unfortunately still more of an art than a science. There's certainly no cookbook process. Even those experienced in the field have differing opinions of the best way to approach such a thing or if it should be attempted at all.

Earthbound spirits are here for many reasons. Some may be lost or confused while others are more aware of their situation and may be seeking some sort of assistance. Still others are perfectly content with their situation and have no desire to cross over. For whatever reason, they feel they need to be here. We need to respect that.

When you attempt to help spirits cross over you are trying to give them a better understanding of their situation and helping them find the path to the other side. You aren't *making* a spirit cross over. You couldn't if you wanted to. You're simply trying to convince them to make that choice for themselves and helping them accomplish the goal if that is their desire.

When a spirit asks for help, we don't usually know what sort of assistance they are asking for. They may be seeking to end their stay on our earthly plane or might simply have a message for someone or are looking for a loved one.

A medium is often helpful in such situations. If they are able to learn why the spirit stayed they have a much better chance of convincing them that it's time to go. Without such help it's often a one-sided conversation with the spirit in hope of hitting the right buttons. But it's still worth a try and can in fact be very successful.

Anything you might have learned about the spirit, either through research or the investigation, could increase your chances of success. Whether it's a name or a clue to when they lived or who they were, any personal information might help you to connect to them. Weave any such knowledge into the script below as best you can.

Another source of support is those on the other side. Our own spirit guides can often be useful in the process if we call on them to help, as can angels and other spiritual beings. The loved ones of the earthbound spirit are also supposedly ready and more than willing to assist but are somehow restrained unless the spirit seeks them.

There are many methods suggested by those who claim to be successful in this sort of thing. All are a bit different, but there is also much commonality. The methods suggested here are based on some general themes as well as my own experiences.

If you meditate, and especially if you call on your spirit guides during meditation, this may be your best approach for a setting within which to work. Begin by bringing yourself into a very relaxed state. Imagine a tranquil setting, either a clearing in a forest or a quiet bay or lakeside in the evening light. Add a few comfortable chairs to your mental image. I use a big cozy chair I can curl up in for myself and a few extras for the spirits I'm trying to cross over. I also have two more formal wingback chairs for my spirit guides, should they choose to join.

In my own visions the chairs are in a semi-circle around either a small campfire or a low round table with several white candles and anything else I might deem relevant. You can choose any setting you're comfortable with. With your eyes closed and maintaining a state of deep relaxation, begin the process of talking to the spirit, inviting them to join you in your circle.

Another option is to find a nice quiet time and place in the home. An area with more activity might work best, but anywhere will do. The evening is a good choice for its darkness and calmness. Set the lights low or turn them out altogether, and add a white candle or any other you may have if you'd like.

If your family is willing, have them join you, but only if they are believers and are truly there to help the spirit. Otherwise try to find a time when you can do this quietly by yourself.

Next, you will need to get in the right frame of mind. Crossing over attempts should always be done with love and compassion. If you're coming from a place of being angry at the spirit for its antics or simply wanting it gone for your own benefit, you're less likely to be successful. Remind yourself that this is the soul of a human being and this soul needs help finding its way.

Now invite any spirits who may be around to join you. Sit quietly for a few minutes to allow them the opportunity to do so. Begin by introducing yourself if you are doing this for a friend and the spirit doesn't know you. If it's your own house you can begin by reminding them that they know you and have shared a home with you for some time.

Explain your intentions and that you are here to help them and mean them no harm. On the following page is a script that I use, although I vary it with each situation. Feel free to modify it for your own needs and in whatever way makes you most comfortable.

I want you to know that I am aware of your presence. Your body died a long time ago but your spirit and your energy are still very much alive. When your body first died you may remember seeing those you love who had passed before you waiting for you in the light. You saw those still of this earth mourning your death. Most spirits choose to go into the light shortly after their passing, but for some reason you chose to remain.

Some people choose to stay because they see the pain that those still living are going through. You can no longer help the people you love by remaining here. You can see that now. Everything has changed and it's time to move on.

Some spirits choose to stay because they are afraid. Some fear that they've done something wrong and will be punished. On the other side you will not find punishment, but instead love, forgiveness, and an opportunity for redemption.

Some spirits are worried that they have left something unsaid or undone. Those are worries that belonged in a time and place that is long gone.

I want you to think about crossing over tonight. I am here to help with that process. There is nothing that is holding you here

any longer. This physical world has nothing to offer you and you must realize by now that you no longer belong here. You are released from any ties that hold you here.

Now I want you to think of how you were as a child. Remember how sweet and innocent you were? Any mistakes you may have made in your life were part of this earthly learning experience. The child that you were is your true spirit. Let that spirit be free to go home now.

Remember your parents and those who loved you? They are waiting for you on the other side. I want you to focus now on those you loved when you were of body: your parents, your grandparents, your sisters or brothers, your spouse, your children, your friends. Look for them now, waiting for you on the other side. Think of them and they will come and help you in the transition.

You are a good spirit and you, yourself, are filled with the light. The light is pure and cleansing. It heals and makes whole. It is now time to go back into the light from which you came. Your time here is over and now you can rest. Love and peacefulness await you. You are released from this world. Go now. Go into the light and you will be home.

Now, pause for a few moments of silence... Picture your caring and compassionate energy lifting the spirit upward toward a pure bright light, not pushing but supporting, as if raising a healed bird in your hands to allow it to again fly free.

As you finish, break the silence slowly and calmly. You may feel a lightening of the energy in the room — if so, that is a sign that you may have been successful. However you may not feel anything and may not know if you were successful right away.

If the activity continues over the next few days simply speak the words of the crossing ceremony out loud as a reminder, or perform the entire process again. It may take several attempts for them to make the decision to cross over, or they may choose to remain here for whatever their reason. Between attempts, however, ignore any activity as best you can and refrain from talking to or acknowledging them, other than your attempts to get them to cross.

Section Two:

They Live With Ghosts!

As much as we can learn about ghosts from current research and theories, there's an aspect of living with hauntings best portrayed through the stories of those who have done just that. For every ghost tale, there is another story: that of the people who live through the experiences and whose lives are often forever changed as a result.

In the following chapters you will be introduced to four families living with one or more ghostly presences through an up-close and personal view of their experiences. Each story is as individual as the ghosts themselves, and each will be different than what you may be experiencing, yet you will likely notice some common factors.

All of these cases are ones for which I have personally acted as the case manager and which have undergone one or more paranormal investigations resulting in some fascinating evidence to support the families' claims. In working with these families, I have also developed a friendship with each. They have all generously agreed to allow me to share their stories in hopes of helping others who find themselves experiencing the unexplained.

Chapter Nine

A Beckoning Home

"All that we see or seem is but a dream within a dream."

— *Edgar Allan Poe*

Jeff and Maria live in a beautiful, late 1800s home in Woodbury, New Jersey, with Maria's two adult sons, her brother, and multiple ghosts. The structure still has most of its original architectural features, and Jeff and Maria have decorated the place with a myriad of antiques layered with casual Victorian touches, Maria's own artwork, and other unique items to give the place a welcoming feel that echoes with whispers and stories. When you walk into the home, you want to stay and listen.

This particular story actually began years before the couple found their historic Woodbury home — or maybe the home found them. When Maria was still married to her first husband, she was going through a difficult time in her life. She had lost both her parents to cancer within a year and a half and, in the months that followed, things got even harder. One night, while lying in bed, she heard a voice in her ear telling her to spy on her husband. ...

The tattletale voice had apparently thought there was something she should know, so late one night she got out of bed and did just that. During our interview, Maria explained that she only mentioned this incident for background...as it was the first of several voices she has heard over the years. The next "voice" was the one that directed her towards the home she's in now.

I was, as usual, recording the interview. While playing it back and typing up my notes, I wasn't at all concerned that Maria had been hearing voices. Given what I knew of her and the home, it just wasn't all that surprising. What was interesting was that just as she spoke of a voice directing her towards the house she's in now — a bit of foreshadowing in the tale she is unveiling — a soft male voice can be heard saying, "Oh yeah." It was as if the unseen gentleman was agreeing, "I certainly did say that."

Maria continued, explaining that after spying on her husband her marriage began to dissolve. As it did, she started to rethink her future and somehow knew she wanted to find an older home in which to rebuild her life. Although she'd never lived in such a home before, she'd always been attracted to items with some age and character to them. She started her search right away, but for two years every house her patient realtor showed her was just not the right one. Her current husband, Jeff, who was listening quietly as Maria shared their story, attested to this fact. He and Maria had started dating sometime during the house hunt and he had been dragged along through showing after showing.

At one point in her search, with aggravating issues stemming from the divorce and the sale of her old home, Maria had gotten very depressed and thought she might never get the home she dreamed of. Again, the voice came through, this time while she was in the kitchen. It said very clearly "Check Woodbury."

In her years of searching, Maria had never looked in this particular town, partly because she didn't think she could afford it. She called her realtor who promptly found two homes for sale in the neighborhood in her price range. Whatever force was driving her to her current home was getting her closer. An hour later her realtor called back with the news that one of the two homes had just been sold that evening. One down, one to go.

Maria arranged to see the house the next day, but she was anxious and decided to check it out that evening. The owners were outside in the garden as she drove slowly by the home. The older couple noticed her and waved, and Maria instantly felt beckoned to both the couple and the home. She describes the feeling that overtook her as odd, as if time had warped and was moving in slow motion.

A welcoming red gate beckons visitors through the side garden.

The dining room, dressed here for Halloween, welcomed Maria on her first visit to the home.

Maria got to the showing a few minutes before Jeff did the next evening. She followed the realtor through the welcoming garden and into the dining room of the historic house. As soon as she entered, she felt so at home that she knew she was going to buy the place.

By this point Jeff had done the house tour drill with Maria many times. When he got to the Woodbury home, the gentleman owner met him at the front gate and escorted him into the dining room to join Maria. As soon as Jeff entered, he looked at the room, looked at Maria, and knew this was the place she had been searching for.

The house was by no means perfect. There were cracked windows here and there and other minor issues, but generally it was solid. To make the sale work Jeff and Maria needed to have the owners agree to be out in thirty days. Throughout the whole sale, the older couple was very accommodating. Maria found out later that

they had apparently been waiting for the right person to entrust their home to — and they had decided Maria was that person, passing over other offers in the process.

The move itself went smoothly, but it wasn't long after that odd things started to happen. At first it was the kitchen appliances. The refrigerator began having issues almost immediately. After that went, the others followed, one by one, each having some sort of critical difficulty. Although the wiring in much of the place was old, the kitchen's electrical system had been completely redone. Still, within six months, they had needed to replace each and every appliance, but, as unusual as that was, it certainly didn't have the couple thinking their house was haunted.

Not long afterwards, Maria started hearing the sound of furniture moving over hardwood floors from the third floor above her bedroom. Her oldest son, Kevin, had taken over the third floor attic, which consisted of two rooms and a closet. The room above her bedroom was carpeted and wouldn't account for the hardwood dragging sounds. Maria thought it was odd that Kevin was constantly moving things around at all hours of the night, but he was a teenager — odd things were to be expected.

One night the sounds were louder and went on longer than usual. The following morning she finally had to ask Kevin what in the world he was doing up there moving furniture at all hours of the night. Kevin calmly reminded her that he'd been away overnight and had just then returned.

At that point Maria had no doubt the house was haunted. She wasn't at all afraid, though; she has never felt fear in her home, she explains. She called the previous owners and mentioned to them that she was hearing odd things in the house — did they have any unusual experiences there themselves? They didn't seem surprised by the question, and yes, they had odd things happen too.

After Jeff and Maria had been settled in the home for a few years, they started doing a bit of renovation. As is common in such situations things got a little stirred up. One morning Maria's younger son, Greg, heard what sounded like someone jumping up and down on the floor of his brother's room above him and called Kevin on his cell phone to complain. Kevin had been sleeping and the call woke him up. On another occasion Kevin was heading up the stairs to his room when he heard a voice saying "Get out!" He quickly complied.

Kevin keeps all of the electronics in his room unplugged. It's apparently necessary to keep them from turning on at all hours. When he first moved in his friends would come over and the lights would sometimes go off and on by themselves. Once they jokingly asked the ghost to turn them off for them again — and it immediately did

just that. Another time a basketball that Kevin kept in the same spot for years came rolling into the middle of the room, maneuvering around the sofa and coming directly towards him. He tried for a day to debunk the incident, but with no luck.

The closet in Kevin's room has a single light socket hanging down from the ceiling. One day he found the bulb unscrewed and on the floor. He put it back in and the next day it was on the floor again. It so happened that an electrician was coming that day to check out the house. When the man examined the old wiring in the closet, he told them that it was a good thing that the fixture didn't have a bulb in it...because the wires were shorted and it could have caused a fire.

The fire theme seems prevalent amongst the odd activity in their home. The original stove that came with the house had caught on fire. Soon after they replaced it Maria was in the kitchen when she heard the click-click-click sound stoves make when you're trying to light the pilot. They were so worried they unplugged it and now light the pilot manually.

Another time Maria had candles lit on the front porch. She was in the back of the house when she heard a voice warning her to check them. Running out front she found a fire had started and the flames were already three feet high. Luckily she got there in time to prevent a catastrophe.

Maria has several times awoken to the smell of smoke during the night and thought the house was on fire. Jeff awoke once to the smell of a dinner being cooked downstairs. Maria has also felt someone touch her while in bed and once awoke to what sounded like a woman whispering in her ear. She has bouts of bad dreams and nightmares and once saw a shadow next to her side of the bed.

The inviting front porch may have burned down had a disembodied voice not warned Maria of the fire.

A sensitive who had been visiting once mentioned that they had felt a little girl spirit on the front stairs. At Christmas one year they were having an open house as part of a neighborhood event. Maria noticed that it was almost time for the activities to begin so she suggested that Jeff watch the front door. He jokingly replied that the girl on the stairs could watch it. Just then a small Christmas tree positioned near the bottom of the stairs fell over. Apparently she wasn't amused.

At the time Maria and Jeff contacted me for an investigation, they had lived in the home for seven years and had become quite accustomed to whomever was there with them. To them, the spirits were simply part of who and what the house was. Still, they were curious to learn a little more, and the most recent incident had piqued their interest even further.

The power had been out one night and Kevin awoke just as it was coming back on to see a man standing and watching him in his bed. The apparition was completely solid and wore knickers, a white wig, and colonial garb that Kevin pointed out predates the late 1800s home. Kevin closed

Maria's paintings of her sons adorn the stairs where a girl's spirit is thought to play.

his eyes, hoping the man would disappear, but he didn't. Finally the gentleman turned and walked into the other room.

An EMF sweep was done as part of the investigation. As with many houses with older wiring, the levels at Jeff and Maria's were significantly elevated. High EMF levels can act as an energy source for paranormal activity. They can also cause feelings of being watched, which might explain what Maria had often felt while in the basement. It didn't explain, however, the many EVPs captured during the investigation or the two light anomalies my video camera caught on the front stairs where the child was thought to play.

The sensitive had shared one other impression with the couple — that someone had been hanged in the home. During the investigation, I sat on the sofa in the living room with my good friend and cofounder Mike Pabian and asked if anyone there had committed suicide. Mike followed with a name of a former homeowner from his historical research. Almost immediately we felt a cold overtake us, mostly over Mike, and for me only on the left side of my body, the side towards him. Several minutes later the cold slowly subsided. I mentioned how the cold had started with my reference to the suicide and it immediately picked up again. This time I felt it move over my hand before it finally subsided altogether.

Although there were several interesting EVPs captured that evening, my favorite was one I recorded shortly before midnight while I was up in Kevin's closet. I asked the resident spirit "Could you touch me?" I felt nothing, but on playback of the recording a man's voice poses the question, "Pleeease?"

Jeff and Maria love their home and I would venture to say that their home loves them, too. Either the house, or perhaps the unseen occupants, seemed to have known the previous owners were moving on and had hand-picked their successors. I don't see Jeff and Maria moving out any time soon, but when the time does come

I can't help but wonder if someone else in some nearby town will hear a little voice suggesting "Check Woodbury."

What We Learned from This Case...

Jeff and Maria are the proud owners of the quintessential haunted home. Its age and location in a town ripe with Revolutionary War history make it a likely candidate for at least some lingering residual energy. Because much of the wiring is older, there are also higher than usual EMF levels in many parts of the home. Whether this has amplified the energy of spirits already there or attracted some nearby locals, we simply don't know.

The activity in their home is typical of a haunted house: sounds of furniture being moved, electronics coming on by themselves, appliances having issues, even occasional disembodied voices. Although the spirits in Jeff and Maria's home can be unsettling at times, especially the one residing on the third floor, the family has come to accept their ghostly roommates. They are simply part of the house — a part that was there long before they were.

Photos in this chapter are courtesy of Debbie McGee.

Jeff and Maria's dog hides under the bed when unseen company comes out at night.

Maria's artwork is sometimes inspired by the house — and very much seems to belong there.

The wine room in the basement gives not even a hint of the occasional paranormal activity within its walls.

An orb above the haunted third floor bedroom window of Jeff and Maria's home.

Chapter Ten

Friend? If Not…
Goodbye!

"Then away out in the woods I heard that kind of a sound that a ghost makes when it wants to tell about something that's on its mind and can't make itself understood, and so can't rest easy in its grave, and has to go about that way every night grieving."

— *Mark Twain*

Our second case involves some of the most varied and amazing manipulations of electronics I have seen. Again we have multiple spirits, with a young girl and an older gentleman determined to be present. The girl, I believe, is quite friendly. The gentleman, whether meaning to or not, has caused a bit of trouble along the way. I'm getting ahead of myself, though… Let's start at the beginning.

As any good ghost hunter will tell you, when a family complains of a haunting, you start with the history of the house itself. If that yields no tale of death or tragedy, you look to see if maybe a purchased or inherited antique is the source of the ghostly spirit — or possibly the family is simply experiencing a friendly visitation from some crossed-over relative. However, there are times that the house, the possessions, and the passed-on family members have nothing to do with it.

Thus appears to be the case with Nobby and Ellen's home in Cedar Run, New Jersey. Nobby built the house himself some eighteen years ago, so its history is well known. Nothing has happened there to make one think it might be haunted. In fact, the home is more solidly built than most, beautify decorated with a comfortable artistic seaside feel, and immaculately kept. It's not a home that even hints at the possibility of being haunted. Yet it is, and very much so.

The setting, too, is perfect; rural suburban America, tucked away on a cul-de-sac with other beautifully maintained homes and backing up into the privacy of the woods. Well, maybe I should be more specific. Not just woods, really: The New Jersey Pine Barrens…the woods of Jersey Devil fame. Now this isn't a story about the Jersey Devil, but these Pine Barrens are the source of many stories, told and untold, and the area is stained with a history of satanic rituals and devil worship.

As you cross Nobby and Ellen's front porch, any hint of negativity you may have picked up on the ride there is immediately washed away. The home is beautiful and comfortable, the couple warm and welcoming, and their two Golden Retrievers complete the homey feel. Not exactly what you might expect from a haunted house.

Nobby had lived alone in the home for several years before marrying Ellen, and from a paranormal perspective those years were uneventful. It was only after his new bride moved in that odd things started to happen.

Ellen is likely the reason they came. She has a history of being around paranormal activity throughout her life and may be a bit psychically sensitive, although she doesn't describe herself that way. In any case, the spirits seem to like her and when she arrived a couple of the locals seem to have sensed that the welcome mat was out. Apparently they decided to make themselves at home.

As with most hauntings, the unusual activity in this otherwise quiet home didn't start with a single dramatic event that screamed "Honey, we have a ghost!" Instead it was many little unexplainable things that over the years left the couple with no other conclusion.

Nobby and Ellen noticed early on that much of the unusual activity would run in cycles. It was as if the ghost would learn a new trick and then repeat it over and over for weeks, even months at a time, just as a young child might tell the same joke over and over until learning a new one.

Initially it was the smoke alarms. Nobby had installed the alarm system himself and, as with all his other work, it was done right. The devices had functioned flawlessly for years. Then suddenly the batteries were constantly being drained, often in the middle of the

The living room television, sound system, and iPod® docking station are among the resident spirit's favorite playthings.

night, resulting in that annoying chirp they emit with a low battery warning.

The alarm in the attic seemed to be the worst offender, with the batteries constantly needing replacement. Nobby even kept a large bag of spare batteries in their bedroom to make the middle of the night changing a bit quicker. He eventually gave up and switched out all of the smoke alarms in the home, replacing the one in the attic twice. The unusual battery drainage continued on briefly before finally subsiding altogether. It hasn't happened since.

Apparently the unseen entity had developed a taste for electronics and was on a roll. The next cycle of nighttime activity involved Ellen's iPod®. The music player was usually left in a docking station on top of the television, which in turn was wired into the stereo sound system. To turn it on not only did the iPod® need to be powered up, but the docking station

and the stereo receiver did as well. So, you can imagine the couple's surprise the first time they awoke in the middle of the night to hear the device blasting music through the stereo system — and not just any music, but dance music, Ellen's favorite playlist.

After the first such incident the couple made doubly sure to check that all of the devices were off before bedtime each night. Yet continually, between three and four in the morning, all three devices would be turned on and the dance music would commence regardless of what had last been played. One night Ellen was tired of the routine and desperate for sleep. When she was awakened yet again to the blaring music, she shut everything off, took the iPod® out of the docking station, and tossed it on the kitchen counter. In the morning it was still on the counter, but was back on and playing away.

Eventually their unseen friend grew bored of the musical game. Again, in the middle of the night they would be awakened to loud sounds coming from downstairs, but this time it was from the television. Apparently their ghost was as picky about its programming choices as it was about its song selection, always tuning into reruns of "The Honeymooners." The show had been Ellen's favorite growing up; the star, Jackie Gleason, reminded her of her father.

Are you starting to get the picture? Whomever was there seemed to, very much, like Ellen or at least wanted her acknowledgment. By repeatedly playing her favorite music and childhood show, it was almost as if to say, "See – I know you – we could be friends."

This playful spirit with a late-night appetite for entertainment was likely not the same one Ellen encountered one night. She awoke to see a large black mass at the foot of her bed. It moved from left to right and then crouched, giving her the impression that it was going to jump onto the bed with her. As would most of us, Ellen screamed. Apparently this did the trick. It disappeared immediately and for the next few weeks things were very quiet.

Another odd sighting occurred when the couple had a visiting contractor. Ellen was in the kitchen with the man when he asked if she had a cat. He had apparently felt something rub against his leg and looked down to see a dark shape go quickly by. No, they didn't have a cat and their dogs had all been outside at the time.

All of this might be enough to make another couple put up a "For Sale" sign, but Nobby and Ellen had always managed to coexist with their unseen roommates fairly contently — at least until one of

Luna and Mac hesitate before joining us in the basement. In fact, Mac avoids the basement whenever possible.

their spirited house guests crossed the line and started messing with their oldest dog, Mac. Mac would begin each evening sleeping peacefully on the floor, but would wake up in the middle of the night, often between 3 and 4 a.m., whining and crying. He would wind up on the bed, under the covers if he could manage it, cowering and shaking until morning and costing the couple a good night's sleep.

It was after many such nights that Nobby and Ellen decided they needed help and called in a paranormal investigation team — thus began my relationship with this wonderful couple. The below "diary" is my rendition of events as taken from e-mail and text exchanges between me and Ellen over a period of eight months.

Mac apprehensively watches the yard from the back porch.

February 18th

Last night Mac got upset earlier than usual, around 10:45. He was actually crying. I awoke to hear not only his whining, but also footsteps in my bedroom, walking at the bottom of my bed toward the bathroom where Mac was. Poor Mac jumped into the bed crying and whining, crawled in between Nobby and me, and I had to pet him for an hour to calm him down. Even then he was still shaking a bit.

February 23rd
(shortly after our "Prelim" visit)

The night after you were here I heard the loudest bang downstairs in the middle of the night, so loud that if I had heard it again I was going to wake up Nob for fear someone was breaking in. It was as if someone threw something on the floor hard, but in the morning nothing was out of place. Then, around 3 a.m. our other dog, Luna, stood at the bedroom door and actually growled into the hallway. She NEVER does that. *(later that day)* My son is visiting and I was just now reading him our e-mail exchange about what happened the other night. Just then we all heard a very, very loud crinkling sound in the kitchen, like someone crunching Doritos® in a bag or something. We all stopped talking and were a bit freaked out.

February 28th

Two really "ruff" nights in a row (couldn't resist–LOL!). Mac was up all night. Last night upstairs he stared at nothing, barking. It was a mean 'I'm-going-to-bite-you' bark.

March 1st

We had to leave our bedroom last night around 1 a.m. and sleep in the living room. Mac started early, and we just couldn't have another sleepless night. He was much quieter downstairs.

March 6th
(the morning after the investigation)

Well, I am excited to see what you guys find. It seemed quiet last night to me. Although I felt like it was around, it seemed as if it was being coy. We slept in the living room last night and very early this morning we heard three loud knocks. We went to the front door thinking someone was here, but nothing.

March 7th

Mac woke Nobby up after midnight last night. Nob heard a loud, continuous tapping sound from downstairs, almost like heavy water dripping on a hardwood floor at a constant pace. He got the flashlight and went downstairs, but it stopped before he was all the way down. He was a bit uneasy so he just went back to bed.

The next morning I tried recreating the sound by knocking on different doors while he was upstairs listening. When I tapped on the closet door across from the bathroom, he said that was it. A few hours later I was vacuuming and noticed the finial from the closet hinge pin right there on the floor. If you tap it on the door, it makes the same sound he heard.

Note: Two nights before, during the investigation, we were talking about an event at another location involving door hinges…

March 11th

I'm afraid we might need to go the route of trying to get rid of whoever is here. We kept asking it to leave us be last night — Nob had to be up at 4 a.m. — but it was a rough one. The night before last I heard a very loud noise in our room, like metal clanging on my mirror or my rosary being swung onto the mirror very hard.

March 16th

We have been sleeping downstairs because Mac hurt his leg and wasn't able to go up. We are going to try and sleep up there tonight, though. We haven't heard anything since the last night we slept up there, but that night there was a very loud bang or thud in the attic.

March 27th

We are back to sleeping in the living room. Something odd has been happening, though. The living room has been filling up with smoke and it freaks us out. Nob gets up and checks the fireplace, but nothing (and we have fires in there all the time with no smoke problem). So we open doors and turn on fans and try to clear the place out. By the morning it's gone. It happened again last night just as we turned off all the lights and shut off the TV, ready for our nightly living room camp-out. As soon as we said something about it, there was a loud noise from the kitchen.

The smoke had a very distinct smell, like a beef jerky being smoked like we've mentioned Nob has smelled before, but this is a hundred times stronger. The first night I could both smell and see it a bit. After that it was just the smell.

Today we were gone for the day and when we got home the ceiling fans were on. We never even turn those on — only some floor fans.

March 30th

Last night I was sitting on the love seat watching TV and Mac started staring just above me and whined like he does upstairs. He went on for a good four or five minutes — he just wouldn't stop. Finally Nob grabbed his camera and snapped some shots and darned if that smoke wasn't above us. Three minutes later it was gone and Mac was fine.

April 4th

We had family over and we all camped-out in the living room together. I was sound asleep when I felt three, hard distinct pulls on the corner of my pillow; it was 6:37 a.m. It was as if she was saying "wake up!" After you were here for the Reveal the other night, I talked to her like she was right there with me. I told her I would let her stay, but only if she would be still at night and just come out and play during the day. I guess she listened!

April 6th

As I was e-mailing you earlier this morning, I heard a very loud static noise upstairs. I stopped for a second, but all was quiet again so I continued typing. Then I heard loud breathing and sighing coming out of my laptop's speakers! I hit "send," turned off the speakers, and had a very stern talk with whoever it was. I must say I'm a bit stressed right now. We may need to do something — I don't like this type of behavior.

The next day I received a text from Ellen that things had gotten worse. She was avoiding her bedroom altogether, choosing to use the outside shower instead of her own bathroom. I went over that night and made an attempt to crossover any willing spirits and then smudged the entire house…or so I thought.

April 9th

Last night was quiet. Although I feel the house is lighter, I feel someone is still here — maybe her?

April 11th

Things have been quiet…

April 19th

Things have been very, very quiet… I hear noises now and then when I am here and it's quiet, but we are sleeping upstairs again and Mac sleeps all night.

May 10th

I had my boys over for dinner and we were talking about you; after they left, Mac started acting odd and looking up a lot. Nob took some pictures and there was that smoke again. No smell at all though.

I commented back that I wondered then if it was the guy spirit who bothered the dogs and he took a hike when we did the smudging. The girl seems to still be around and is fine around the dogs.

That is what I think… that she stays all the time and he was the troublemaker and is gone… for good maybe?

An odd smoke appears in a photo of Mac shortly after he was acting oddly.
Photo courtesy of Nobby and Ellen.

May 12th

I came downstairs this morning and my cell phone screen was on the Internet, on my Facebook page. I am on Facebook all the time, but I have only accessed it on my phone once in the last two years. Anyway, I hollered at Nob, thought he was snooping on my phone, LOL... and don't ya know, I was home alone, painting a new painting on the porch, nice and quiet. I had my cell phone on the table next to me and I noticed the screen light went on. I thought I was getting a text so I looked over at it and actually watched as it went on the Internet all by itself. Weird, huh??

June 17th

I think the guy is back. We're hearing noises in the garage — I even recorded some on my phone. I left it in there recording and when I listened back it sounds like someone is in there moving around. The other day all the surfboards fell, as if they were slid off the racks.

Apparently there was a second attic above the garage that we missed and didn't smudge... It appears as if the male spirit may have been holing up in there for a few months. I came back and did a second smudging, but before I did, I conducted a mini-investigation with Ellen and Nobby. During the first investigation, we got a very clear EVP of the girl saying "I like you" in the basement so I wanted to start down there.

As the three of us headed down the stairs, I was saying how I hoped the girl would talk to us again. Apparently she was with us already — on playback her voice joins in with our stairway conversation saying "Let's go down!"

We concluded our investigation that night in the attic above the garage where we all experienced a sustained cold spot. I then gave the house a thorough smudging, including the second attic this time.

June 25th

Last night Nob was on the back porch with a visiting family member. I was outside and about to come in, but was no where near the door yet. Mac headed out the doggie door, as he always does, but this time the screen door opened forcefully inward, against the springs, and hit poor Mac right in the face. The guys both saw the door open by itself right in front of them!

June 27th

I was looking at some old pictures and just remembered one incident. I had just swept the living room rug and turned around to unplug the vacuum. When I turned back there on the floor was a large box of fireplace matches that had been on the mantle just a second ago. It freaked me out so badly that I grabbed a camera and took a picture. That was two years ago...

This morning I was out running errands and I had the radio on playing music as always. It started to scan through the channels, as if someone had pushed the seek button, but the same original station kept playing. It was nuts. I turned the radio off, waited, and then turned it back on again — it did the same thing. I tried another station and that one played, but it was still scanning — it reminded me of the Frank's Box you used during the investigation. I pulled over, hit record on my phone, and started asking questions. Just then there was a loud bang on the car as if a rock was thrown at the windshield.

June 28th

Our almost new refrigerator — the one that backs to the garage, ha ha ha —

An odd streak of light appears in a photo of Ellen. A few nights later she witnessed a similar light anomaly coming out of the ceiling of her master bedroom. *Photo courtesy of Nobby and Ellen*.

has been acting up. The repairman came today and apparently it's shot.

July 12th

I was just in the kitchen and Nobby came in and said I looked pretty and wanted to take a picture of me. When he checked it, he saw this bright white snaky light thing. Is it her or maybe him? I would say "yes." *The couple tried to recreate the effect using a hair on the lens with no luck. Nothing they tried was even close.*

August 7th

Hey, I wanted to tell you… two nights ago I was in bed watching TV and I saw the same thing like we got the picture of… a long really bright light that flashed down from the ceiling. It looked like a very fat illuminated snake!! Freaked the crap outta me!!!!!!

August 11th

Nobby finally heard something — a male voice in the kitchen — while he was making breakfast. Me, I have not heard or seen anything since the glowing snake thing.

September 1st

I was in the house all afternoon, playing my iPod® really loudly, and then I turned it off to put on the TV news. Remember how the iPod® docking station and the TV are connected to the same sound system? Well, the ghost turned the music back on! Five times now we've been back and forth with it — it's insane!!!!

September 9th

My team did another investigation of the couple's home and, during this second investigation, we captured both the little girl and a male, although there may have been more than two voices. In male voices, we got the names "Barry" and "Dawson" in different parts of the home.

The little girl also came out clearly, as she always seems to do when I record there. At one point Ellen asked if she should leave the room. A soft voice replies "no" and another follows with "Mommy."

At one point in the evening I was coming up the basement stairs. When I reached the exact spot where I had previously captured the girl saying "Let's go down," I received yet another message from her. This one broke my heart. It simply said "Help."

September 29th

I heard her really loudly last night. It's been fairly quiet, but last night I was watching *Ghost Hunters* (LOL) lying in bed and was thinking about her. Half an hour later there was a really loud bang at my nightstand — as if a large animal had jumped onto it knocking into my lamp and jewelry box. I looked over, startled, and of course nothing was there. Ha ha ha — like I thought there would be? *(later)* She's messing with Nobby's phone now. It won't work inside the house — the screen goes crazy and won't stop scrolling. He can't text or make calls, and a friend who was over with an iPad® couldn't get that to work either.

September 30th

Hey, I think I saw her today. I was on the front porch blasting my music and doing a painting and singing and a shadow darted between me and the wall, right behind the lamp I had on. I actually thought it was a darn bird it was so dark and so fast. Just thought I would share!

October 2nd

She had us up last night. Her new favorite place seems to be next to my bed by the nightstand. I get awakened by clanging often and Mac was growling right afterwards.

October 16th

Something really weird happened. I want your take on it. The only thing I did on my PC this morning before leaving for the day was to look at the CD you guys gave us from the investigation. When we were leaving, I told Nob of three bad dreams I had last night, one right after the other, all about something or someone bad trying to hurt me and I could not get away. He said maybe we should just call a priest

A shot of the actual message Ellen found written on her computer when she logged into Facebook one evening. *Photo courtesy of Nobby and Ellen.*

and get rid of these ghosts, they may be negative spirits... and then we went to a party all day.

I just got home and opened up my Facebook using my bookmarked page, so I did NOT type anything. Yet there was this phrase typed into my search engine, and it's not anything I have ever typed, and it's my PC. Nobby never uses it. It said "Friend? If not...Goodbye! If u do." That was it!! Could they be doing this to my PC?

I was doing yard work yesterday and had an empty trash can next to the one I was filling with leaves, and something actually kicked the trash can — loud. It was arms length from me. Your thoughts?

What We Learned from This Case...

With Cedar Run, we have seen a haunting that is not associated with the history of the home itself. At least one of the spirits there is very active and is constantly learning new tricks and finding new ways to communicate. As we often see, the activity here is focused on the woman of the house, although the man gets his fair share as well, and even visiting friends and family are subject to some playfulness.

Also, as with many hauntings, when the odd activity began, the couple had no idea what was causing it. It took many such incidents to start the couple thinking that they might be sharing their home with a ghost or two. When they called in a paranormal investigation team, they already knew they had spirits — they just needed some help finding out more about what was going on in their home and getting whatever was there to stop harassing the poor dog so they could sleep.

We have also seen how spirits can get attached to the living as the little girl here has with Ellen. Whether she is confused and sees Ellen as her mother or if she's simply adopted Ellen as such, she has become Ellen's little shadow.

The activity at Nobby and Ellen's has never been directly threatening, except possibly to their dog Mac (and we really don't know if what spooked him was intentional). Even though the couple has been very open to sharing their home with a couple of ghosts — as long as they behave and follow the rules — there have still been times when their experiences have been less than pleasant. Still, overall, it has offered them an amazing first-hand view of the paranormal. Many of us watch the ghost hunting shows and wonder. Well, Ellen and Nobby watch them and know.

A Curious Enigma

One interesting finding from our investigation remained an enigma as we put the case file together for the Reveal. I had a recorder on the kitchen counter and when the room was empty, with the investigators on other floors of the home and the couple sitting quietly on the back porch, I captured maybe half a dozen unexplainable loud knocks in the room. Mike was the Lead Investigator and while visiting the couple for the Reveal he set out in search of the source of the bangs.

What he found was quite curious: The couple's home has a small bathroom near the entrance to the garage and directly across from the closet that had mysteriously lost its hinge pin finial. The toilet in the bathroom is modeled after the old-fashioned sort that flushes with a pull cord hanging down from a tank set up high. Although the knob on the end of the pull cord doesn't sway with normal flushing, if one were to force it to swing, it would hit the wall with a bang exactly like the kind we had heard. Interestingly enough, the paint and drywall were worn in just the spot it would hit, as if someone had been repeatedly doing just that.

The morning after this discovery Nobby applied a layer of spackle to the indentation before heading off to work.

Ellen was upstairs and hadn't gone in the bathroom at all until she came down a few hours later to clean it. She instantly noticed a small ding in the damp spackle, and a dab of soft spackle on the wooden end of the pull cord.

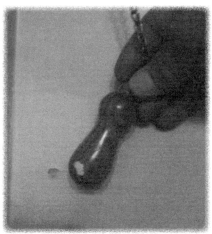

Top: The pull on the toilet cord must have hit the wall many times to make these impressions in the paint and drywall.
Bottom: A fresh coat of spackle wasn't about to stop the ghosts little game.
Photos courtesy of Nobby and Ellen.

Chapter Eleven

Mr. Grumpy Pants

---

*"Many human beings need no supernatural mentoring
to commit acts of savagery; some people are devils
in their own right, their telltale horns having grown
inward to facilitate their disguise."*

— Dean Koontz, Odd Thomas

Both the Woodbury and Cedar Run cases are more typical of an active haunting. Although there were occasional incidents that were unnerving or upsetting, for the most part, the activity wasn't negative. This next case from Groveville, New Jersey, is not quite so pleasant.

When I first met Raymond and Marsha, they lived in a small apartment with Marsha's twelve-year-old daughter McKenzie. Their building was over 150 years old, the two-story structure having originally been built to serve the nearby textile mill. It was now divided into apartments, with Raymond, Marsha, and McKenzie occupying a lower unit.

At first things had been fine in their cozy home. Then the landlord began renovating the apartment above them, tearing the place down to the studs in the process. As soon as the construction began, some very negative energy took out its frustrations on the apartment below — and its residents. By the time Marsha sought the help of a paranormal investigation team, the renovations had been going on for three or four months and things had gotten quite bad. Her investigation request read:

"We have experienced whispering, moaning, shadows, tugs on our clothes, dreams that wake us up, scratches, pinches, welts, knocks, things falling or moving, and a hand print on my bathroom mirror at my work, like it followed me. We can't sleep at night, even sleeping with the lights on they still come out. We think there are many different types of spirits here, small children, bigger ones, men, and women..."

An odd handprint appeared out of nowhere on the mirror where Marsha worked. *Photo courtesy of Raymond and Marsha.*

When I first contacted Marsha, she had wanted me to call her while she was at work. She was worried that even talking about them on the phone might further aggravate them. In most cases that wouldn't be something I'd be concerned with, but this was definitely not like most cases and caution was warranted.

During our first conversation, Marsha told me of how one night she awoke to the feeling that someone was sitting on the bed with her. Her dog, Precious, was quite old and typically slept through everything, but whatever was cozying up to her had gotten the dog's attention as well — and Precious's growling made it clear that whatever it was wasn't welcome.

Marsha also shared that one of the spirits would follow her on occasion. Once, while driving to work, something gave her seat belt a hard yank. Another time a handprint appeared on the mirror at her work. When she considered sleeping in her car to escape the nightly harassment, she quickly realized that it would likely follow her there as well.

McKenzie, was having a difficult time as well. She had frequent nightmares and her bunk-bed would shake convulsively at night. Oddly, during the investigation there were above-baseline EMF levels on her top bunk. There was no apparent source for the anomaly; as the meter was moved in any direction away from the mattress, the EMF levels would return to normal.

Marsha was troubled by the whispers she would hear in her bedroom, but that was the least of it. Her hair would be pulled while she was doing the dishes — once hard enough to tilt her head back. Sometimes an unseen hand would lightly touch the small wispy hairs in front of her ears — and she was constantly being awakened between 2 and 5 a.m. by some unseen cold energy. Lately, she explained, it was aggressively right up in her face.

We often see heightened paranormal activity when someone in the home is psychically sensitive, as these people tend to draw the attention of earthbound spirits. This case is no different. Marsha is an Intuitive and an Empath. She can often pick up emotions from people and has learned to block these feelings at times so as not to be overwhelmed. She also can tell when spirits are around her and sense their emotions as well.

Marsha had done what she could on her own before calling for help. She tried sage; it helped for a day or two, but the activity came back stronger. She tried asking them to stop; they ignored her. She put a crucifix over her bed and tried prayers from several religions; once, after she had said the prayers, "it" growled in her ear.

As much as Marsha and McKenzie were experiencing, though, Raymond was largely left alone. Maybe there was something about him that kept the spirit at bay. While that was likely part of it, the dominant male spirit in the home clearly seemed to have a strong preference for females. However, Raymond was still there for Marsha and did what he could to protect the girls — no matter how far-fetched Marsha's psychic impressions sounded to his skeptic self.

By the time I had heard all of this, I was obviously concerned for the family. This was one of those cases where you need to do something to get things under control before worrying about an investigation. The first place to start is by usually having the client talk to the spirit, or spirits in this case, and firmly lay down a few rules. In Marsha's case, the lack of sleep was the biggest issue so I wanted her to start with that. I asked her to begin by telling the spirits that they needed to stop disturbing her and her daughter at night...that if they wanted to express themselves they would need to do it during the day. They were no longer allowed to bother her family while they slept.

Marsha began taking control immediately. I figured when I spoke to her the next time I could have her add a few more rules to her daily lecture. No need. Once she learned what to do, she was off and running, setting ground rules left and right — and it was working! The energies had backed off; at least enough to let her and her daughter get some sleep at night. Whoever was there was far from gone, though. McKenzie's bed was still shaking and there were other signs the spirits were around, but things were much better and finally tolerable. Once, as Marsha was laying down the ground rules yet again, she heard a loud moan. I took it as a good sign. I could just picture the spirit thinking, "Oh my God, here she goes again with all the rules! Can't a ghost have any fun?"

By the time I visited Raymond and Marsha for the Prelim, the activity was much more under control and we were ready to get down to business. Marsha explained that she believed multiple spirits were present with a dominant male leader that she later came to refer to as Mr. Grumpy Pants (a very kind nickname for this not-so-kind spirit). She felt they were associated with the mill nearby. Often, when she returned home from work, several spirits would take notice and leave the mill to join her. Maybe they had lived in the house previously and were also returning home at the end of the day or, possibly, they were just drawn to

Marsha. Other times Marsha would sense spirits coming into her apartment from the upstairs unit that was unoccupied and under renovation. She believed they used a stairway that led to her master bedroom — a stairway that no longer existed.

After our initial tour, Marsha sensed Mr. Grumpy Pants shushing the others in what she described as a "be quiet or we'll get in trouble" way. Interestingly enough, weeks later when we did an investigation we got an EVP of a male voice saying "Pull back... back...", as if again directing other spirits to remain unnoticed.

Several times during our visit Marsha heard a breath or sensed a presence. At one point she and I were standing together in her kitchen when she suddenly felt Mr. Grumpy Pants right next to her. Oddly I had that hair-standing-on-end feeling sometimes associated with spirit encounters just before she mentioned his presence.

A few minutes later it happened again. This time his presence was unnerving enough to make her almost bolt to the other side of the room. I felt it more strongly as well, over the entire left side of my body this time. When I left Marsha that day, I had no doubt that her "feelings" were right on the money.

One of the more frightening and violent incidents happened not long before I met Marsha. Her older daughter, Katrina, was nineteen at the time and was staying over. For some reason Mr. Grumpy Pants was in a particularly nasty mood one night while Raymond was away. Katrina was walking past the bathroom when she felt a sudden burning, stinging sensation. Marsha lifted her shirt to find scratch marks on her back.

Mr. Grumpy Pants was also up to a little butt-pinching that night. The girls huddled together in Marsha's bed when they'd had enough. When Raymond got home, he snapped a photo as Marsha felt the presence return. In it, an odd bright mist can be seen above them.

They all slept together that night, or tried to sleep as best they could. McKenzie awoke after a vivid nightmare, the events of which took place in that very room. In it she saw a young girl with long dark hair wearing a white nightgown of style worn long ago. The girl was crying and trying to get out a door — a door that no longer existed in the current home.

As the little girl sobbed trying to escape, a man grabbed her, scratched her, and threw her against the wall. The girl's mother entered, covered with cuts, and the man picked her up by her throat and threw her against the wall as well.

That night Marsha felt a strong presence from the empty upstairs apartment. As they had gotten in the habit of doing, Raymond took a picture through the apartment window from outside their building. These photos were often filled with odd shadows and what appeared to be faces. In the shot he took that night, McKenzie recognized the little girl.

Marsha felt a sadness coming from a smaller presence in the home at times. To her that usually indicates a woman or child. She added that she could probably see if it was a child or not if she opened herself up, but that hearing them was bad enough and she was afraid to start being vulnerable to the visions as well so she kept them blocked.

It's possible that the dream McKenzie had that night had been just a dream, with the evening's events fresh in her mind. It's also quite possible that a little girl was

An odd light anomaly appears above Marsha and the girls as they take refuge in bed the night Katrina was scratched. *Photo courtesy of Raymond and Marsha.*

sharing a vision with McKenzie or that she was picking up on a scene played out long ago.

The investigation of the home was quite fruitful. Several light anomalies were captured on video, the sound of footsteps was heard, a bang emanated from an empty room, and there were multiple unexplainable EMF spikes, as well as quite a few personal experiences. Many EVPs were also captured, including the voices of a male, a female, and a young girl.

On one of the breaks during the investigation Marsha mentioned that the dominant male spirit, aka Mr. Grumpy Pants, was angry at our being in the home. The vision she had was of him holding a big boulder over his head and wanting to smash it down on us. She felt that he didn't like the male presences in the home, Raymond or my cofounder Mike, who was on the investigation with us that evening.

Near the end of the evening we asked Marsha to join us in the master bedroom. I was sitting on the floor when she first felt the presence of the little girl enter the room. Marsha felt that the girl was scared and that Mr. Grumpy Pants had hurt her in the room. I spoke to him, telling him that he needed to leave her alone, that she was just a little girl, and he was being a bully. Addressing the little girl, I explained that she could cross over anytime she wanted; she didn't need to stay.

Marsha then shared her impressions: "The little girl was afraid of him. She was looking for the door, but couldn't find it. She was confused and couldn't find her way out. She paused and added, "He keeps her confused."

At that moment, I did something that I don't generally recommend. I told the little girl that she could come home with me. I explained to her that I had a little boy spirit at my house but no mean men. Marsha whispered that the little girl was behind me. Suddenly I felt her — a tingly static feeling over my whole body as I sat cross-legged on the floor. I asked Marsha if that was her. She said yes… The little girl was hugging me.

I told the young girl that I would come get her at the end of the night and that after she was safely home with me I would help her cross over. The next part I wasn't prepared for. Marsha interpreted for the girl: "She wants her mommy to go." Gulp. Two for one night… Of course I told her that her mommy could come, too.

I continued, explaining to the girl that she was allowed to go anywhere she wanted, that spirits weren't stuck in one place and that the man couldn't keep her there. Marsha chimed in that he just made her *think* she had to stay. It was then that I felt her energy back off. Marsha said she'd gone upstairs to get her mommy.

After the investigation concluded, I went back to the bedroom and again invited her and her mother to leave with me. I had the sense that they might have joined me for the ride home, but really I couldn't be sure. Just in case, when I got home, I invited them in and told them to make themselves at home.

For the next few days I waited for any unusual activity to occur in my house, but there was none. One afternoon I was ready to talk to them and I asked my son to join me in an EVP session. I hoped the little girl spirit might be more willing to talk to someone closer to her age. As I spoke to her on that sunny afternoon in our kitchen my son saw an orb a few feet in front of us and felt her presence. She was there.

Soon afterward I tried to help her cross over. We felt nothing of her after that. I can't say I ever did sense her mother or knew if she was ever there at all. I checked in with Marsha now and then, almost afraid to ask each time if the little girl and her mother had been around. They hadn't. Old Mr. Grumpy Pants was still there, though, and wasn't too pleased about losing his girls. One day, about a month or so later, Marsha told me of another dream McKenzie had. She once again dreamed of the little girl, but this time she was happy and playing. It was just the sort of dream a crossed-over spirit might share.

Things were fairly quiet, or at least livable, in Raymond and Marsha's place after that — until the landlord started a final round of construction in the upstairs apartment. Marsha was again unable to sleep well and felt a slap across her face awakening her one morning. Everyone was having bad dreams and McKenzie would wake up during the night to a different little girl and someone saying "Hehehehehe" in an evil sort of a laugh.

The rest of the story will need to be left for the next family. Raymond, Marsha, and McKenzie moved out. Hopefully Mr. Grumpy Pants will be attached enough to the mill to remain behind and, when the construction is finally over, maybe he will once again be able to rest.

As with other sensitives, Marsha and McKenzie will likely always have occasional visitors. They will need to keep their blocking skills polished. As time passes, their memory of the events in that home will hopefully fade, but I'm fairly certain they will never be forgotten.

What We Learned from This Case...

Given everything negative that was going on in the home, especially the scratching, pinching, and the growl, my first concern was that whatever was there might possibly be demonic. Luckily the evidence in this case does not support that.

First, the activity began with construction, which is common with earthbound spirit hauntings. All of the women in the family were subject to the attacks, so it wasn't centered on just one individual as we often see in demonic cases. It also didn't escalate the same way that demonic cases usually do; there were no putrid smells and no one was overwhelmed with feelings of anger or hatred. Although not all demonic cases have such symptoms, the lack of them here was a good sign.

The other indication that we weren't dealing with a non-human entity was that when Marsha began laying down the house rules and being quite firm about it the spirits for the most part cooperated. You won't find demons giving up quite so quickly. More than anything, with Marsha's gifts, I trusted her interpretation of the energy. She had no trouble calling it evil — and who wouldn't — but it was definitely human.

Mr. Grumpy Pants is not a spirit I would ever choose to share a home with, but I'm betting he wasn't a very nice guy when he was alive either.

Chapter Twelve

Peace for a Sensitive

"The most beautiful thing we can experience is the mysterious."

— *Albert Einstein*

I must admit, I might never have become a ghost hunter if I had known in advance I would be going though people's houses, laying down the rules with their ghosts, burning sage, ringing bells, giving out crystals, spraying saltwater, and instructing people on energy grounding and protection techniques. I'm an engineer — such things weren't even in my vocabulary.

Then I became a case manager with a paranormal investigation team. I was the one who worked with new clients when they called for help. An investigation can be a big part of the solution and in many cases is all that is needed. However, when a client isn't sleeping through the night or is worried for their children, just telling them that a team will be out to investigate in a few weeks, and we should have the results a few weeks after that, well... that sometimes falls more than a little short of what they need.

Each case is different, and with each case I needed to learn a little more. The paranormal community is a fantastic resource — there is no shortage of help out there and I'm indebted to those from whom I've learned. Mark Johnson, the Founder of my first team, New Jersey Paranormal Research, started me down this road by teaching me how to have the clients take control verbally. Mark is extremely knowledgeable in the paranormal so I certainly didn't doubt him when he suggested the technique for my first desperate clients. I shared it with them with pure conviction, but I must admit I was just a little surprised when it actually worked.

With each case in need of help, I would add another technique to my arsenal and, with each addition, I questioned my own sanity a bit more. I wasn't making these things up, though — they each had some basis in success, many in centuries of success, at least theoretically. Maybe all of these were simply psychosomatic solutions; if I believed they would work, if I could be convincing with the client, then maybe that was enough. I decided in the end it really didn't matter — that if anything could be done to make the client's situation better, then it was worth a try, no matter how ridiculous I looked.

When it came time to help one particular client, I pulled out all the stops, weaving everything I truly believed into one carefully orchestrated plan. I had come to believe that crazy or not, the plan might just work. In this case it simply had to, but let's start at the beginning.

Vinnie and Liz live in Hillsborough, New Jersey. I was first introduced to them after Vinnie submitted an investigation request online. They were experiencing knockings often and other activity on occasion. The television, lights, and a ceiling fan would turn on and off, a smoke alarm blared for no apparent reason, their dachshund would constantly stare into the master bedroom closet or corner growling, and the sound of someone walking upstairs could be heard when no one was up there.

As with many women in similar situations, Liz had been having significant trouble getting a good night's rest and, as with many men in similar situations, Vinnie usually slept just fine. On my first visit to the home, Liz recounted how a few nights prior she had awoken in the middle of the night to see a jolly fat man standing naked at her bathroom sink, the flab of his belly resting on her countertop. He was wearing a shower cap and was busily brushing his teeth when she spotted him. Liz stared for a second — she had to use the facilities and this was a bit of a dilemma — and he shot back a dirty look that quickly convinced her she didn't need to go quite that badly.

Given all of the activity in their home, and especially this one particular visitor, Liz was taking it all fairly well. It wasn't too surprising — she was actually quite used to it. Liz is a bit of a sensitive and a medium. She's never been formally trained and has never used her gift in any professional capacity. Messages from the other side have just always come to her, often in flashes or knowings, or sometimes she just gets people's names. I also tagged Liz as a bit of an Empath. She seems to easily receive emotions from people and spirit encounters often leave her depressed, saddened, or upset. She had never learned to block these spirit energies and they were now taking advantage of the situation a little too often.

It was clear from the start that the activity in the home revolved around Liz. She had mentioned in our initial interview that she would deal with certain frustrations by writing them in her journal, yet, when she did, the activity in her home would pick up. That can often be a sign of psychokinetic activity, similar to the poltergeist phenomena, where the human mind and emotions can affect our physical environment. However, given her psychic gifts, it seemed likely that more was going on.

During my first visit to Vinnie and Liz's home, we did the usual tour. In the master bedroom, Liz explained how the room would sometimes feel heavy, as if underwater. We worked our way through the rest of the house and finished our conversation in the living room. Before leaving I felt drawn to go back upstairs and sit in the master bedroom for a bit. Fortunately I had my recorder with me because my experience was a little more than odd and listening back to it helped me confirm my own recollection.

In the upstairs hallway, I announced, "You're here. I feel you." I am not one who is all that sensitive so that was an unusual thing for me to say. A moment later I was approaching the threshold into their bedroom. Although the door was wide open, I was literally stopped in my tracks. Well, not quite stopped — it was more like I was bounced back into the hallway.

I took a breath, not sure what had just happened, and tried again. Once again I was stopped. It was as if the room was filled with a bubble of energy that I couldn't break through. Now I was catching on and I was determined. I leaned my head forward as one might when heading into a windstorm and literally pushed my way into the room. This time the force yielded. As soon as I made it past the threshold, the energy lightened up a bit, but the room still felt heavy.

On my recorder, the event sounded a little less ominous. I was tagging as I went, as usual, so on the recording you can

Liz stands just inside her bedroom door. An hour later an unseen force prevented me from entering the room.

hear me say, "I'm heading into the master bedroom," and then a pause and a deep breath before I continued, "Okay, I'm *trying* to head into the master bedroom…"

An investigation was definitely in order and was conducted by New Jersey Paranormal Research, my team at the time. The events, mostly knockings and flashlight activity, did seem to be focused around Liz, but there were also a few EVPs that further convinced me that it wasn't just her.

My belief was that Liz was an open doorway to many spirits, some familiar to her and others not. To get the situation under control would require a two-pronged approach: Cleanse the home and teach her the energy skills needed to close her psychic doorway, at least for now, with the goal of having her be able to open and close it at will as she became stronger.

The compounded effect would, hopefully, be cyclical. If the cleansing helped lessen the activity, even temporarily, Liz could sleep. If she could sleep, she would regain her strength and her defenses would become stronger. This, in turn, would help her to keep the activity at bay.

It made sense to get Liz working on closing off her energies first. Otherwise any clearing we were able to accomplish could be quickly undone. When I first met Liz, I wasn't well versed in energy work, but by the time she asked my newly founded team, Paranormal Consulting & Investigations of New Jersey, to come help her get things under control I had found just the ticket. I happened to be reading *The Ghost Hunter's Survival Guide: Protection Techniques for Encounters with the Paranormal* by renowned medium Michelle Belanger and had found myself writing Liz's name in the margin the day before she called me for help. I ordered the book for her and let Michelle do the teaching.

The next step was to give Vinnie and Liz's home a good smudging. Pat Kibby, my good friend and cofounder, had been on the investigation and volunteered to accompany me. Sweet optimistic Liz greeted us with open arms, as always, but the dark circles under her eyes were probably the most significant I'd ever seen. Things had escalated and she was unable to sleep through the night. Unseen forces would awaken her between 3 and 4 a.m., causing her to abandon her bed and seek refuge on the living room sofa, reading or otherwise keeping herself occupied, so her husband might get his rest.

We began with an attempt at crossing-over any spirits who might have been ready to take that step. Next, I lit a sage smudge stick and poked my head up into the attic crawlspace while Pat used my tingsha cymbals to loosen up any negative energy. We worked our way through the house pushing the smoke out the front door and then finishing up in the basement, pushing that smoke up and out as well.

Usually I would have been content with that, but in Liz's case we needed a little more. I left her with a small quartz crystal to keep beside her bed with instructions to cleanse it with sea salt periodically. It reminded her of a similar crystal her beloved Puerto Rican mother, Lucy, had possessed, which helped strengthen its significance. I also left her with some lavender incense to burn every night before bed. Part one was done.

Liz had been doing her part as well, reading Michelle's book and practicing the energy and protection techniques. Pat made another key observation. By letting the spirits chase her out of her bed every night, Liz was giving them control.

Pat used the analogy of when our kids start getting a little older, but still sneak into our beds in the middle of the night. At some point, we need to take control and claim the bed as our own. Pat asked Liz to do just that — to hold her ground and not get up between 3 and 4 a.m., not even to use the bathroom. She needed to reclaim her territory. Hopefully the smudging would help make that task easier, but if she didn't hold her ground we might just be back there smudging again in a few weeks.

Pat and I left Liz and Vinnie with the usual hugs and high hopes. We knew she could do it — would do it. Still, we thought about her often over the next week, wondering how she was getting along. My clients are always free to call me at any time, but I try to refrain from calling them for a week or two after a cleansing at the risk of stirring up anything that may have been somewhat settled.

Finally, a week later, I gave Liz a call. I almost didn't recognize the voice on the other end of the line. It was the same sweet optimistic Liz, but she now had so much energy and happiness emanating from her that I could feel it right through the phone. She explained that things had gotten much better right away. There was some minor knocking at first, but much less than usual and the spirits were finally leaving her alone at night. She was doing her energy work each day, lit the incense each evening, and had reclaimed her bed.

Most importantly, Liz was finally sleeping again, which, in itself, can be a life-changer. She felt happy, she exclaimed, and said she would catch herself laughing again. She was back in control of her life and well on her way to making sure things would stay that way. She also noticed that her dog, Princess, was much less anxious and was even playing again, certainly another good sign.

I checked in with Liz a few weeks later and things were still good. Yes, there was still some occasional knocking on the walls, "but there always will be," she said without the least bit of concern.

It always amazes me that there are people out there with gifts such as Liz's. These gifts aren't always easy to live with. Liz and Vinnie are amazing people and the opportunity to have had them in my life was a blessing.

I have one last thank you for Liz. When I first visited her home, she gave me the name of someone on the other side that had come through for me, as she is often given communication through names. It wasn't a name I recognized at the time as anyone I had known. Months later, while talking to Liz on the phone, the name came to her again, but, again, I had no clue who this spirit might be.

At the time, I hadn't yet read the story that identified the ghost from my childhood as "Margaret." Although decades have passed since I had shared my home with her spirit, I have thought of her often. It is largely because of her that I ventured into the world of the paranormal, a journey that has brought so much fulfillment to my life.

Yes, the name Liz gave me was indeed "Margaret." It was wonderful to know that she hadn't forgotten me, either.

Liz and Princess are both happier now that the
activity in their home has subsided.

Afterword

The four stories you just read about these families and their hauntings are probably on the active end of the scale in terms of what is typical. Many families live with much quieter ghosts, although some do have spirits that make the ones in this book look boring.

Occasionally people will become quite attached to their ghosts, even considering them to be part of the family. As with family, spirits can be frustrating at times and some can be easier to live with than others. If you do find yourself sharing your home with a spirit, try to remember that it is simply a human being who is no longer human, but is definitely still being.

With hauntings, as with life in general, the greatest fear is often the fear of the unknown. Hopefully this book has shed some light on the world of ghosts and the paranormal and has helped you to feel a little more comfortable about the possibility of sharing you home with an unseen entity. Maybe you will even begin to appreciate the glimpse they give us into the world beyond what we see and hear everyday: the world of the paranormal. Once your eyes are open, there is so very much to see.

"There is a mystery to that which is invisible to the living, when only our senses tell us something is there. I wonder if spiritual travelers don't engender memories within us of recognition of what we once were and will be again."

-- Michael Newton, Pd.D.
Destiny of Souls: New Case Studies of Life between Lives

References

On-Line Resources

Ananda, Psychic and Card Reader
anandasword@gmail.com

Burlington County Prison Museum
http://www.prisonmuseum.net

Chip Coffey, Psychic, Medium, & Spiritual Counselor
www.chipcoffey.com

Empire Antiques
www.empireantiques.com

Ghost Tours of New Hope
http://ghosttoursofnewhope.com/

Haunted-Gettysburg.com
"Haunted Places in Gettysburg," accessed Nov. 11, 2011
(www.haunted-gettysburg.com)

John Zaffis, Godfather of the Paranormal
www.johnzaffis.com

Paranormal Consulting & Investigations of New Jersey
www.pcinj.org

Phenomenalog
www.phenomenalog.com

PSYORG.com
"Young children learn to tell fact from fiction," accessed Dec. 4, 2006
(http://www.physorg.com/news84473786.html)

Rasmussen Reports
http://www.rasmussenreports.com/public_content/lifestyle/holidays/

United Paranormal International
http://unitedparanormalinternational.ning.com

World Paranormal Investigations
www.wpiusauk.com

Book Resources & Recommended Readings

Balzano, Christopher. *Picture Yourself Ghost Hunting*. Boston, Massachusetts: Course Technology, 2009.

Belanger, Michelle. *The Ghost Hunter's Survival Guide: Protection Techniques for Encounters with the Paranormal*. St. Paul, Minnesota: Llewllyn Publications, 2009.

Bertoldi, Concetta. *Do Dead People Watch You Shower?* New York, New York: Harper, 2008.

Coffey, Chip. *Growing Up Psychic: My Story of Not Just Surviving but Thriving and How Others Like Me Can, Too*. New York, New York: Three Rivers Press, 2012.

Danelek, J. Allan. *A Case for Ghosts: An Objective Look at the Paranormal*. St. Paul, Minnesota: Llewllyn Publications, 2006.

Edward, John. *One Last Time: A Psychic Medium Speaks to Those We Have Loved and Lost*. Berkley, Michigan: Berkley Trade, 1999.

Fiore, Edith Dr. *The Unquiet Dead*. New York, New York: Ballantine Books, 1987.

Hoffman, Steve. "Music Hall bones studied." *Cincinnati Enquirer*, May 14, 1988.

Jeffery, Adi-Kent Thomas. *Ghosts in the Valley*. Westland, Michigan: Hampton Publishing Co., 1971.

Jeffery, Adi-Kent and Lynda Elizabeth Jeffery. *Haunted Village & Valley*. Stockton, Kansas: Rowe Publishing, 2010.

Morris, Tom Ph.D. *Philosophy for Dummies*. Foster City, California: IDG Books Worldwide, Inc., 1999.

Newton, Michael Pd.D. *Destiny of Souls: New Case Studies of Life between Lives*. St. Paul Minnesota: Llewellyn Publications, 2009.

Newton, Michael Ph.D. *Journey of Souls: Case Studies of Life Between Lives*. St. Paul, Minnesota: Llewllyn Publications, 1995.

O'Donnell, Elliot. *Twenty Years Experience as a Ghost Hunter*. Bournesmouth, England: W. Mate & Sons, LTD., 1916.

Plato and Erich Segal. *The Dialogs of Plato*. New York, New York: Bantam Books, 1986.

Righi, Brian. *Ghosts, Apparitions and Poltergeists: An Exploration of the Supernatural through History*. St. Paul, Minnesota: Llewllyn Publications, 2008.

Rojo, D. Scott. *On the Track of the Poltergeist*. San Antonio, Texas: Anomalist Books, 2005. (Originally published by Prentice-Hall Inc.)

Roll, William G. "About Poltergeists." *American Society for Physical Research Newsletter*, No. 26, 1975.

Stevenson, Ian. "Are poltergeists living or are they dead?" *Journal of the American Society for Physical Research*, July 1972.

Van Praagh, James. *Ghosts Among Us*. New York, New York: HarperCollins, 2008.

Vanden Eynden, Rose. *Ask A Medium*. St. Paul, Minnesota: Llewllyn Publications, 2010.

Winkowski, Mary Ann. *When Ghosts Speak*. New York, New York: Grand Central Publishing, 2009.